W9-BAQ-104

Volume **5**

THE GOLDEN BOOK ENCYCLOPEDIA

concerto to dynamite

An exciting, up-to-date encyclopedia in 20 fact-filled, entertaining volumes

Especially designed as a first encyclopedia for today's grade-school children

More than 2,500 full-color photographs and illustrations

From the Publishers of Golden® Books

Western Publishing Company, Inc.
Racine, Wisconsin 53404

ILLUSTRATION CREDITS
(t=top, b=bottom, c=center, l=left, r=right)

1 r, David Lindroth, Inc.; 1 lf, Michael O'Reilly/Joseph, Mindlin & Mulvey; 3 br, Craig Aurness/Woodfin Camp; 4 all, Juan Barberis/Artist Network; 5 tr, New York Public Library Picture Collection; 5 bl, David Lindroth Inc.; 6 t, Jim Pickerell; 6 inset, Paolo Koch/Photo Researchers; 7 and 8 tl, Marilyn Bass; 9 tl, David Overcash/Bruce Coleman Inc.; 10 and 11 b, Juan Barberis/Artist Network; 11 tl, Federal Energy Management Program/ U.S. Department of Energy; 13, Tom Powers/Joseph, Mindlin & Mulvey; 15 br, Michal Heron/Woodfin Camp; 15 t and 16, David Lindroth Inc.; 17 tl, Tom Powers/Joseph, Mindlin & Mulvey; 17 br and 18 tl, David Lindroth Inc.; 18 b, Tom Powers/Joseph, Mindlin & Mulvey; 19–21, Mei-Ku Huang, M.D./Evelyne Johnson Associates; 22 b, James M. Cribb/Bruce Coleman Inc.; 24–25 t, Mei-Ku Huang, M.D./Evelyne Johnson Associates; 25 br, National Optical Astronomy Observatories; 26 br, Michael O'Reilly/Joseph, Mindlin & Mulvey; 27, Tom Powers/Joseph, Mindlin & Mulvey; 28–29 t, Gary Lippincott/Publisher's Graphics; 28 bl, © Joe Viesti; 28 inset, Culver Pictures; 29 inset, Junebug Clark/Photo Researchers; 30 tl, John S. Flannery/Bruce Coleman Inc.; 31, Crosby Pulliam/Photo Researchers; 33, Gary Lippincott/Publisher's Graphics; 34 b, David Lindroth Inc.; 34 rc, Gary Lippincott/Publisher's Graphics; 36 br, Kim Taylor/Bruce Coleman Inc.; 36 inset, Dr. E.R. Degginger/Bruce Coleman Inc.; 37 rc, Wendy Whiriss/Woodfin Camp; 38, Culver Pictures; 39, The Thomas Gilcrease Institute of American Art and History, Tulsa, Oklahoma; 40 rc, Susan McCartney/Photo Researchers; 41 David Lindroth Inc.; 42 tl, Neal & Molly Jansen/Shostal Associates; 43, Bill Ross/Woodfin Camp; 44 and 45 tl, Tom Powers/Joseph, Mindlin & Mulvey; 45 tr, Adam Woolfitt/Woodfin Camp; 45 c, Tom Powers/Joseph, Mindlin & Mulvey; 46, © Joe Viesti; 47, Loren McIntyre/Woodfin Camp; 48 tl, Historical Pictures Service, Chicago; 48 tr, Sandy Rabinowitz/Publisher's Graphics; 49, Martha Swope; 50, Bettmann Archive; 51, Dennis O'Brien/Joseph, Mindlin & Mulvey; 52, Brad Hamann; 53 br, Sven-Olof Lindblad/Photo Researchers; 54 tr, Weyerhaeuser Company; 54 bl, Dennis O'Brien/Joseph, Mindlin & Mulvey; 55, The Museum of the Confederacy; 56, Tom Powers/Joseph, Mindlin & Mulvey; 57 tl, David Lindroth Inc.; 57 tr, Kurt Scholz/Shostal Associates; 58 tl, Jim Brandenburg/Woodfin Camp; 58 br, Frank Mayo; 59 br, Independence National Historical Park Collection; 60 tr, John Rice/Joseph, Mindlin & Mulvey; 60 b, Jack Couffer/Bruce Coleman Inc.; 61, The Photo Source; 63 tl, Marilyn Bass; 63 br, Delaware Development Office; 64 tl, Fred Mayer/Woodfin Camp; 64 br, Bruce Roberts/Photo Researchers; 65 tr, Blair Seitz/Photo Researchers; 65 rc, Courtesy of Dr. Robert Herbin; 66 tr, Bettmann Archive; 67 tl, UPI/Bettmann Newsphotos; 68 bl, Richard Frear/National Park Service; 68 br, Tom McHugh/Photo Researchers; 68 t, David Lindroth Inc.; 70, David Lindroth Inc.; 71 t, © Joe Viesti; 71 inset, Michael O'Reilly/Joseph, Mindlin & Mulvey; 72 t, Manfred Kage/Peter Arnold, Inc.; 72 inset, Smithsonian Institution Photo No. 78-8853A; 73 tl, Reprinted with permission of the publisher from the *Macmillan Dictionary For Children,* Revised Edition (back cover), © 1975, 1976, 1977, 1981, 1982, 1987, Macmillan Publishing Company, a division of Macmillan, Inc.; 75 br, Norman Myers/Bruce Coleman Inc.; 75 t, Randy Taylor/Sygma; 75 inset, Van Phillips/Leo de Wys Inc.; 76 tr, Ron Seguin/Dr. Dale Russell/National Museums of Canada; 76–77 b, Robert Frank/Artist Network; 78, E.R. Degginger/Bruce Coleman Inc.; 79, Bettmann Archive; 80, David Burnett/Contact/Woodfin Camp; 81 tr, Akhtar Hussein/Woodfin Camp; 82 and 83, Michael O'Reilly/Joseph, Mindlin & Mulvey; 84, David Lindroth Inc.; 85 bl, Baron Wolman/Woodfin Camp; 85 br, Richard Hutchings/ Photo Researchers; 86 all and 87 br, Lisa Bonforte/Evelyne Johnson Associates; 87 bl, Michael Freeman/Bruce Coleman Inc.; 88 tl, H. Armstrong Roberts; 88 br, Norman Owen Tomalin/Bruce Coleman Inc.; 88 t inset, The Brooklyn Children's Museum; 88 b inset, John Rice/Joseph, Mindlin & Mulvey; 89 br, David Lindroth Inc.; 89 rc, Martin Rogers/Woodfin Camp; 90, UPI/Bettmann Newsphotos; 91, Illustration from *Aladdin and the Wonderful Lamp,* © 1987, Anthony Aocardo, used by permission of Western Publishing Co., Inc.; 92, Susan Leavines/Photo Researchers; 93, Frank Mayo; 94 c, Reprinted by permission of *Weekly Reader,* published by Field Publications, copyright © 1987, Field Publications; 95, C. Max Dunham/ Photo Researchers; 96 tr, Bruce Lemerise/Joseph, Mindlin & Mulvey; 96 bl, Bernard P. Wolff/Photo Researchers.

COVER CREDITS
Center: Tom Powers/Joseph, Mindlin & Mulvey. Clockwise from top: © Joe Viesti; Robert Frank/Artist Network; Tom Powers/Joseph, Mindlin & Mulvey; Sarkis Buchaklian; Tom Powers/Joseph, Mindlin & Mulvey; Becky Tachna.

Library of Congress Catalog Card Number: 87-82741
ISBN: 0-307-70105-0

ABCDEFGHIJKL

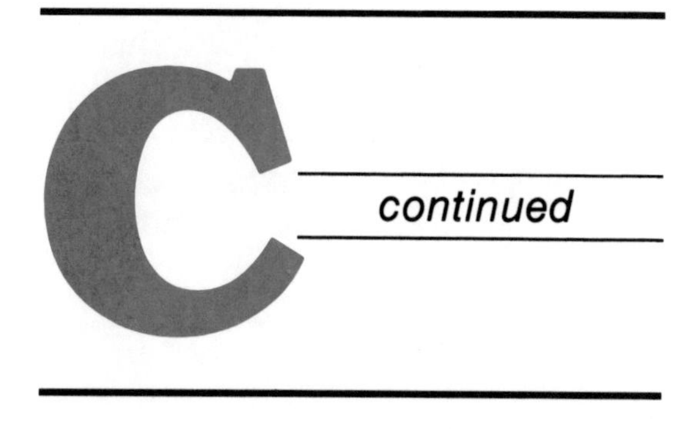

concerto

A concerto (kuhn-CHAIR-toe) is a piece of music written for one or more solo instruments and an orchestra. Symphony orchestras often play concertos at concerts.

Most concertos are written for piano and orchestra. There are also many for violin and orchestra. Concertos have been written for most other instruments, too.

In most concertos, the solo instrument and the orchestra take turns playing the *themes*—the main melodies. When the solo instrument is playing the theme, the orchestra may *accompany*—play along with it in the background.

Concertos usually have three parts, called *movements.* The first and third movements are usually fast. The second movement is slow. Near the end of the first movement, there is often a part called a *cadenza* for the solo instrument alone.

The first modern concertos were written in the late 1700s. Joseph Haydn and Wolfgang Amadeus Mozart composed many concertos. Other famous concertos were written by Beethoven, Mendelssohn, Brahms, Tchaikovsky, and Rachmaninoff.

See also **composers** and **music.**

concrete

Concrete is an inexpensive and very strong building material. It is used to pave highways and to build skyscrapers, bridges, tunnels, dams, and many other things.

Concrete is easy to make. Sand, crushed stones, cement, and water are mixed together. The mixture makes a heavy paste that can be poured into molds, called *forms.* The forms give it the right shape. When it dries, it becomes hard as rock.

The concrete used in buildings or bridges is usually poured around steel rods to make it even stronger. Concrete with steel rods is called *reinforced concrete.* It is one of our most important building materials.

Cement is a major ingredient of concrete. Cement is a fine gray powder made from rock that has been heated and then crushed. It is also used in making *mortar,* the material used to hold bricks or stones together. The ancient Romans used both concrete and mortar for buildings, roads, and tunnels. Many of these still stand. In 1824, an English builder named Joseph Aspiden invented *portland cement.* It is the kind we use most often today.

This graceful highway bridge is made of concrete reinforced with steel.

cone-bearing plant

If you have ever seen a Christmas tree, you have seen a cone-bearing plant. Cone-bearing plants, sometimes called *conifers,* do not have pods or fruits to produce seeds. Instead, they produce seeds in structures called *cones.*

Most cone-bearing plants are evergreen trees or shrubs. They keep their leaves all year. Their leaves are small. Some leaves look as though they are made from tiny scales. Juniper and cedar trees have leaves like this. Other leaves are like needles. Pine and spruce trees have this kind. A few cone-bearing plants are not evergreen. Larches are cone-bearing plants that lose their leaves every year and grow new ones.

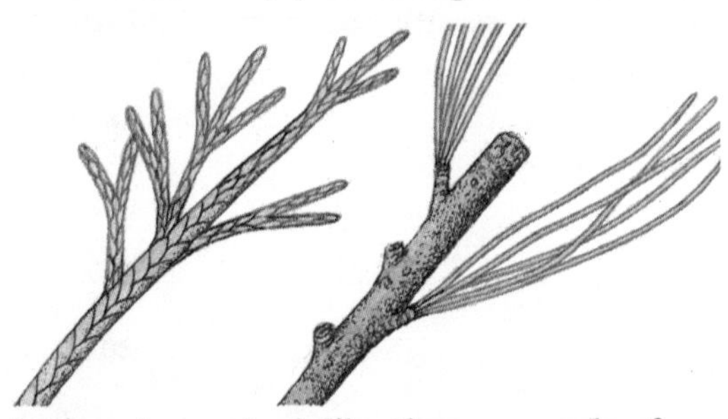

Juniper leaves look like they are made of scales (left). Pines have needles (right).

Cone-bearing plants can stand cold weather and poor soil. They need less water than other plants because they lose less water through their leaves. Huge forests of cone-bearing plants stretch across the cold northern parts of North America, Europe, and Asia.

The cones of most cone-bearing plants are hard and woody. They may be small and almost round, or very long. The cones of the white fir are only 5 to 10 centimeters (2 to 4 inches) long. But the cones of the sugar pine may be more than 60 centimeters (2 feet) long.

Pinecones can be 2 feet long or as small as a thimble.

As pinecones ripen, they open and lose their seeds. These seeds are food for some animals.

When the cones first form, they are tightly closed. The seeds inside them grow slowly, sometimes for several years. When the seeds are ripe, the sections of the cone spread outward. The seeds fall out, reach the ground, and grow into new plants.

The cones of lodgepole pine trees stay closed until there is a fire. Then the cones open with a pop and the seeds are scattered. These new seeds help replant the burned area.

The cone-bearing plants include the largest plants on Earth—California's giant redwoods and sequoias. One of them, called the General Sherman Tree, is 83 meters (272 feet) tall. Measured straight through the middle near the ground, its trunk is 11 meters (37 feet) thick. This redwood tree is one of the oldest living things on Earth. It is more than 3,500 years old! (*See* **redwoods and sequoias.**)

Cone-bearing plants are important to us. Many provide lumber for building. Others provide turpentine and important oils. We plant cone-bearing trees and shrubs near houses and office buildings for beauty and year-round protection from wind and sun.

Confederate States of America

The Confederate States of America were 11 Southern states that *seceded*—broke away—from the United States of America. They left the Union because they thought President Abraham Lincoln would try to end slavery in the South. Their government—often called the Confederacy—lasted from 1861 to 1865, the period of the American Civil War.

In 1860, South Carolina became the first state to secede. Five more southern states—Mississippi, Florida, Alabama, Georgia, and Louisiana—followed in January 1861. Texas left the Union in March. In February, representatives from these states met in Montgomery, Alabama, to plan their government. By May, four more states had joined them—Arkansas, North Carolina, Virginia, and Tennessee. The Confederate states elected Jefferson Davis of Mississippi as their president and made Richmond, Virginia, their capital.

The Confederacy faced major problems. It won a few early battles of the Civil War, but could not keep winning against the Union's strong forces. Other nations did not consider these states independent and would not help them.

The Confederacy grew weaker and finally collapsed. The war ended, and one by one the Confederate states returned to the Union.

See also **Civil War; Davis, Jefferson; Lincoln, Abraham;** and **slavery.**

The Confederate states stretched as far west as Texas and as far north as Virginia.

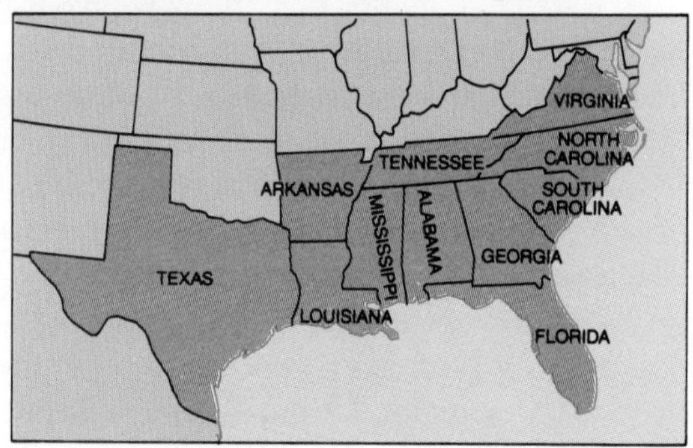

A picture of Confucius done in the 1800s. No one is sure what he really looked like.

Confucius

Confucius was a teacher and philosopher who lived in China between the years 551 and 479 B.C.

The family did not have very much money. But Confucius would not let anything stop him from going to school. He became one of the most educated people in China. He opened a school so he could share what he had learned with others.

Students at Confucius' school studied the Chinese language and literature, poetry, history, and public speaking. They also learned the ceremonies and beliefs of Chinese religion. Confucius taught his students to treat their parents with great respect. He believed that family respect made a nation strong. He said people should be honest, loyal, obedient, and thoughtful.

Confucius' ideas about how people should live are called Confucianism. His advice was collected into books. His ideas became an important part of Chinese life.

Congo, *see* Africa

Above, the two houses of Congress meet all together to hear the president. Usually, the House of Representatives and the Senate meet separately. At right is the United States Capitol, the building in Washington, D.C., where the Congress meets.

Congress, United States

Congress is the part of the United States government that makes laws. It is also known as the *legislature.* The members of Congress are elected by U.S. citizens to represent them—to act for them in the government. Most members of Congress are either Democrats or Republicans—members of one of the two main political parties in the United States. (*See* **political party.**)

Congress is divided into two main parts, the House of Representatives and the Senate. There are 535 members in all. They are called *congressmen* and *congresswomen,* or *representatives.* A representative must be a U.S. citizen, at least 25 years old, and must live in the state he or she represents.

Each representative is elected for a two-year term by the people of his or her *congressional district.* Every state is divided into congressional districts. The number of districts in a state depends on the state's population—the number of people who live there. Some states, such as Alaska, have so few people that they have just one district—the entire state. States with many people, such as California, may have over 40 districts. The number of districts in a state is decided every ten years, after the population is counted by the census. If states gain or lose population, they may gain or lose representatives. But every state must have at least one representative. (*See* **census.**)

The other part of Congress is the Senate. Every state, no matter how many people live there, has two members of the Senate, called *senators.* There are 50 states, so there are 100 senators altogether. A senator must be a U.S. citizen, at least 30 years old, and must live in the state that he or she represents. Each senator is elected for a six-year term.

Congress meets in a building called the Capitol in Washington, D.C. One wing of the Capitol is occupied by the House of Representatives. The other wing is the home of the

Senate. When Congress is in session, visitors to Washington can watch meetings of Congress from a balcony.

At a session of the House of Representatives or the Senate, members make speeches on different subjects. They also discuss and vote on bills. A *bill* is a law that has been introduced but not passed. A bill becomes a law only if it is passed by both houses of Congress and then signed by the president. If the president does not like the bill, he may *veto* it—refuse to sign it. If he does this, the bill can still become a law, but only if the houses of Congress vote on it again. Each house must then pass the bill by a two-thirds majority of those voting.

Each part of Congress has certain powers of its own. Only the House of Representatives can introduce bills that involve taxes. Only the Senate can vote yes or no on officials chosen by the president, such as judges. And only the Senate can vote on *treaties*—agreements between the United States and other countries.

The vice president of the United States presides over—directs—meetings of the Senate. The House of Representatives is presided over by one of its members, called the Speaker. Members of each party choose other officials, too. They work to make sure that members of their own party vote on important bills.

Much of the work of Congress is done outside the two big meeting halls. Everyone in Congress serves on at least one *congressional committee.* A committee is a small group that deals with a certain subject, such as the armed services or farming. Each bill brought before Congress goes to a committee first. If the committee votes against it, it does not even reach the other members of Congress. This saves time, because at least 10,000 bills are introduced every year. Only about 1 out of 20 bills becomes a law.

Committees often hold hearings, at which private citizens or experts in certain fields can speak for or against a bill. For example, a committee may want more information

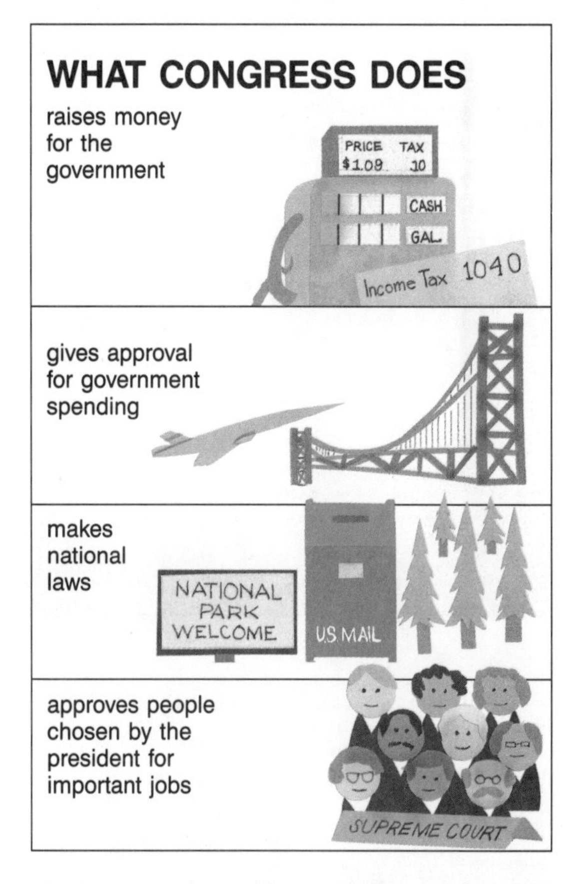

about a bill to help farmers. Several farmers might appear before the committee to say how much the bill would help them. Other people might appear to speak against the bill. They might say, for example, that it would cost too much money.

Each member of Congress has an office and a staff of people who are paid to help. The staff gathers information about issues and bills. Staff members also help answer mail and phone calls.

In a democracy, it is the people who rule. Voters should keep their senators and representatives informed of their problems. In fact, every year, the members of Congress receive a total of over 70 million letters. Sometimes, people want to give their opinions on an issue or a bill. Sometimes, they need help on a local matter, such as repairing a highway or building a hospital.

See also **government; Constitution of the United States;** and **Supreme Court, United States.**

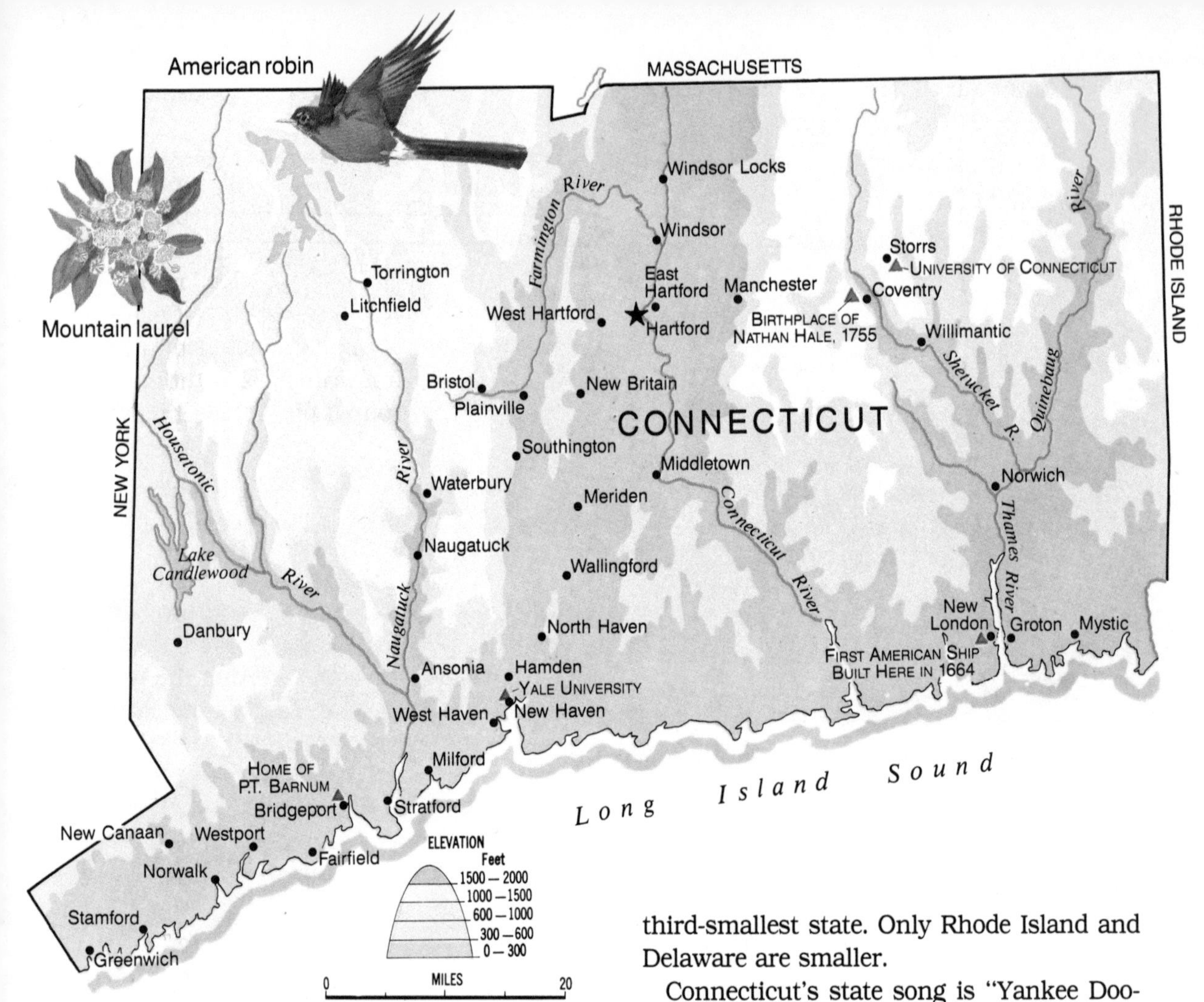

Connecticut

Capital: Hartford
Area: 5,018 square miles (12,997 square kilometers) (48th-largest state)
Population (1980): 3,108,000 (1985): about 3,174,000 (27th-largest state)
Became a state: January 9, 1788 (5th state)

Connecticut was one of the 13 original colonies, and it was the first New England colony to become a state. It is in the northeast corner of the United States and is the third-smallest state. Only Rhode Island and Delaware are smaller.

Connecticut's state song is "Yankee Doodle" and its nickname is the "Constitution State," because it had the world's first written constitution. The name Connecticut comes from an Indian word meaning "beside the long tidal river."

Land and People The Connecticut River enters Connecticut from Massachusetts in the north. It flows south through the center of the state and empties into Long Island Sound, an arm of the Atlantic Ocean. The beaches on the state's southern shore face Long Island Sound. Forests cover more than half of the state. The rest of the land—except for the Berkshire Hills in the northwest corner—is mostly flat, rocky, and not very fertile. For this reason, not much farming is done in Connecticut.

Most of the state's people live in the Connecticut River Valley and along the shore of Long Island Sound. Hartford, the capital city, is near the center of the state, on the river. It is a manufacturing and insurance center. In

An old whaling ship at Mystic Seaport in Connecticut.

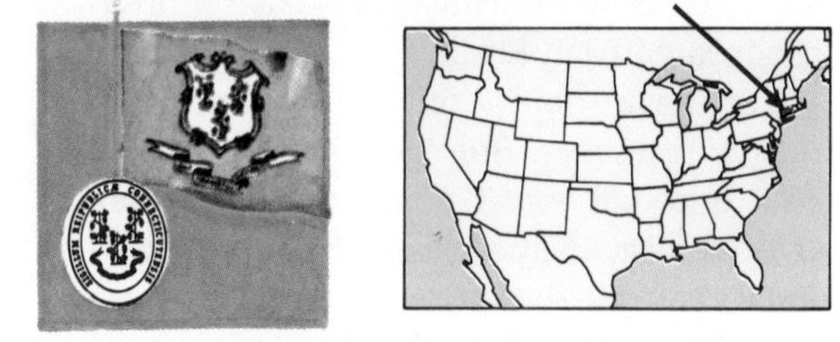

fact, it is known as the "Insurance Capital of the United States."

New London is the most important city in eastern Connecticut. It is on Long Island Sound, and is the home of the U.S. Coast Guard Academy. Near New London is Groton, a U.S. Navy submarine base. The world's first nuclear-powered submarine, the *Nautilus,* was launched there in 1954. East of Groton is Mystic Seaport, which looks like a real whaling village of the 1800s.

About 50 miles west of New London is New Haven, the home of Yale University. Still farther west is Fairfield County, which borders New York State. Many people who live in Westport, Darien, Greenwich, Stamford, and other Fairfield towns travel to New York City every day to work. Others work for General Electric, Union Carbide, Xerox, and many other large companies that have headquarters in Fairfield County. Bridgeport, the state's largest city, is an industrial center.

Most of the people living in Connecticut today were born in the United States. The largest foreign-born group is Italian.

History The first European-American towns in Connecticut were built along the Connecticut River in the 1600s by settlers from Massachusetts. Windsor, Hartford, and Wethersfield formed the Connecticut Colony. In 1639, they drew up the Fundamental Orders, the world's first written constitution. In 1638, another group from Massachusetts sailed down the Connecticut coast and started the New Haven Colony. The colonies joined together in 1665.

Connecticut soldiers fought in many battles of the Revolutionary War. The state also made guns and ammunition, and provided food that helped keep General George Washington's troops from starving. After the war, Connecticut became the fifth state to ratify the U.S. Constitution.

During the 1800s, Connecticut became an important industrial state. Clocks, brass, locks, and guns were some of its products. Smith and Wesson, Samuel Sharps, and Samuel Colt soon made Connecticut the center of the U.S. gun industry. The state produced many of the guns used by the Union Army during the Civil War, and came to be known as the "nation's arsenal"—weapons storehouse. It still makes more helicopters, military aircraft engines, and nuclear submarines than any other state.

Many well-known people have lived in Connecticut. During the Revolutionary War, the state produced a famous hero, Nathan Hale, and a famous traitor, Benedict Arnold. Hale said, "I only regret that I have but one life to lose for my country" just before the British hanged him. Arnold sold American secrets to the British.

Some of Connecticut's famous inventors are Eli Whitney, known for inventing the cotton gin; Samuel Colt, for the six-shooter; and Edwin Land, for cameras that develop their own pictures. Charles Goodyear found a way to treat rubber to keep it from becoming soft and sticky in hot weather.

Harriet Beecher Stowe, a famous writer from Connecticut, wrote *Uncle Tom's Cabin,* about the evils of slavery.

conservation

Earth is home for millions of different kinds of living things. It provides the land, water, and air that these living things need. All these things—land, water, air, plants, and animals—are what we call *natural resources.* So are the many beautiful places on Earth—the lakes and waterfalls, forests and deserts, sand dunes and coral reefs. Other valuable resources cannot be seen. These include coal and oil still buried in the ground. We like to think that Earth's vast resources will always be there for us. But if we do not protect them, they may not be. Protecting natural things from harm is called *conservation.* People who protect natural and living things are called *conservationists.*

Conservationists study all kinds of living things. They also study air, water, soil, and different kinds of land forms, such as mountains and seashores. Groups of people concerned about conservation are found everywhere in the world. The Audubon Society studies and protects birds. The Sierra Club helps protect forests and mountains. The International Wildlife Federation studies and protects living things everywhere. Some world groups are concerned about African land that is turning into desert. Other groups want to protect Earth's energy supplies. Still others are trying to keep the world's rain forests from being destroyed. Plants in these rain forests produce much of the world's oxygen.

Why Conservation Is Needed As humans live and use the earth, we often cause harm. Cars and factories put dangerous gases into the air. Sewage and other wastes can harm rivers and kill fish. Chemicals sprayed or spilled on the soil can poison the land for years. When we build cities, we force wild plants and animals to find new homes. If they cannot find other places to live, they die. Some kinds of living things have entirely disappeared from Earth.

Humans are not the only things that harm Earth's resources. Storms can knock down trees and kill small living things. Ocean waves can eat away a seashore. Erupting volcanoes can fill the air with harmful gases, cover the ground with ash or melted rock, or start giant mudslides. Large meteorites have knocked down forests and set fires. Lightning, too, causes many forest fires.

Plants and animals can survive many natural events. Some of them even need hurricanes or fires in order to reproduce. Other natural events, however, can cause serious problems. Volcanoes, meteorites, or climate changes may have wiped out whole groups of living things in the past.

Ways to Conserve Conservationists look for ways for people to live on Earth without

When trees are destroyed by fire (below), conservationists plant new, young trees. If factories (next page) cause pollution, we look for safer ways to dispose of waste and replace animals that have died off.

This poster shows one way to save heating fuel. Caulking closes cracks around windows and doors, keeping heat in.

destroying it. They teach people ways to prevent pollution of air and water. They work with farmers to find better ways to protect soil from erosion. They also work to keep hunters from killing too many game animals, such as elk and bears.

Conservationists keep track of the numbers of all kinds of living things. When the numbers of any group of living things go down, conservationists try to find out why. If the group's homes are being destroyed, they look for ways to protect those homes. If water pollution is the problem, they try to find the cause and stop it. If the group is in danger of vanishing from the earth, conservationists try to protect it.

One way to protect a group of animals or plants whose numbers are growing smaller is to declare it an *endangered species.* Laws prevent people from collecting or killing an endangered species. Sometimes, an endangered species is moved to a safer place and protected until its numbers increase. This was done with the last few California condors. (*See* **animals, endangered.**)

Protecting special areas on land is an important part of conservation in the United States. These areas are national parks, national monuments, and national forests.

Each protected area has things that make it special. Yellowstone National Park has beautiful mountains and geysers—natural fountains of hot water that shoot up out of the earth. It also has a large herd of American bison, an animal once in danger of being wiped out completely. The Florida Everglades is another protected area. It is a swampy wilderness of saw grass and mangrove trees. Many endangered animals live there, including crocodiles, egrets, and bald eagles. Other protected areas include deserts, seashores, and canyons.

The law says that these areas must be kept in their natural state. People cannot build houses on these lands. Plants and animals living in them cannot be collected or killed. In some ways, visiting a national park is like seeing America as it was more than a century ago.

See also **environment; natural resources; air pollution;** and **water pollution.**

Constantine the Great

Constantine was a Roman emperor who ruled in the 300s—almost 1,700 years ago. By the time he came to power, the Roman Empire was not as strong as it had been. But Constantine was a strong ruler and did much to preserve the empire.

One of the most important changes during Constantine's rule involved Christianity. Rome had a state religion and sometimes punished people for being Christian. But one day, just before an important battle, Constantine had a strange vision. He said he saw a cross, with the words *By this sign you will conquer.* Some say the cross appeared in the sky. Others say he saw it in a dream. Constantine made the cross his emblem. He won the battle.

Constantine himself did not become a Christian until he lay dying. But he allowed Christians to practice their religion freely. Soon, Christianity became the official Roman religion.

In 324, Constantine moved the capital from Rome to a small Greek city near the Black Sea. He enlarged the city and named it Constantinople, after himself. This great center lasted long after the Roman Empire crumbled. Today, it is the city of Istanbul in Turkey.

See also **Christianity** and **Roman Empire.**

constellation

A constellation is a group of stars that form the shape of a person, animal, or mythical creature. Each constellation has a name that usually tells you what it looks like, such as Draco the Dragon, or Pisces the Fish. Often, you need to know what the shape is supposed to look like to be able to see it.

For example, to see the Dragon—Draco—you have to connect the stars with imaginary lines, just as you do in a follow-the-dots drawing. That gives you a general idea of Draco's shape. You can fill in the details with your imagination.

The Greeks and other ancient peoples found these shapes among the stars and named many of the constellations we know today. They even had legends to explain how the constellations were formed. For example, a Greek god named Zeus supposedly created the constellation of stars called Gemini—the Twins—to honor his twin sons, Castor and Pollux.

Astronomers today use the constellations to describe the regions of the sky. Every star, even the ones we can see only with telescopes, is located within a constellation. The stars are named with Greek or Latin letters or numbers, combined with the name of a constellation. For example, the nearest star to Earth is named Alpha Centauri A. It is the brightest star in the constellation Centaur.

Constellations also play a role in astrology. Astrologers refer to 12 of them as the *signs of the zodiac.* (*See* **astrology.**)

Without the aid of a star chart, constellations can be hard to find. As the earth rotates, they appear to move westward across the sky. Some can be seen only during a particular time of year. You must know about where and when to look for the one you want to see. Here are some constellations that are fairly easy to find.

IMPORTANT CONSTELLATIONS

The Great Bear—Ursa Major—can be seen all year round. The Big Dipper is part of the Great Bear and may be the easiest of any group of stars to find.

The Little Bear—Ursa Minor—is nearby but is harder to see. The Little Dipper is part of this constellation. Find the Big Dipper first. Then imagine a line running through the two bright stars at the end of the dipper. The line points up toward the Little Dipper.

The Swan—Cygnus—is also called the Northern Cross. Look for it between June and November. The brightest star in the constellation is part of the swan's head.

The Whale—Cetus—is a large constellation visible between October and January. It appears just below Pisces.

The constellations are groups of stars that appear together in the night sky. Ancient peoples believed that the stars outlined shapes of animals and people.

The Hunter—Orion—is one of the easiest constellations to find in the winter sky. He holds a club in his right hand, and faces Taurus, the bull. Orion has many bright stars, three of them marking his belt.

The Lion—Leo—can be seen between February and June. It is one of the zodiac constellations. Leo is large and fairly easy to find. It looks like a large animal walking along on four legs.

The Virgin—Virgo—is another zodiac constellation. You can usually find it just to one side of Leo from April through June.

The Fishes—Pisces—is a zodiac constellation that can be seen between October and January. It looks like two fish, each on a separate fishing line. The two lines come together at the constellation's brightest star, Al Rescha.

The Bull—Taurus—can be seen between October and March. A cluster of stars form the bull's head.

The Twins—Gemini—can be seen between December and May. It is a zodiac constellation located above Orion. A bright star marks the head of each twin but they are found at the bottom of the constellation.

The Dragon—Draco—is an ancient constellation, found in the Northern hemisphere. It contains no major stars, and is hard to see in the night sky. The dragon's "tail" lies between Ursa Major and Ursa minor.

The Crab—Cancer—is another constellation of the zodiac. It is located between Gemini and Leo, but is not easy to see because it contains no bright stars.

We the People of the United States, in order to form a more perfect union, establish justice, insure domestic tranquility, provide for the common defense, promote the general welfare, and secure the blessings of liberty to ourselves and our posterity, do ordain and establish this Constitution for the United States of America.

The Constitution begins with these words.

Constitution of the United States

The Constitution of the United States is a document that outlines the basic rules by which the country is governed. It also explains the basic rights of all U.S. citizens.

The Constitution was written more than 200 years ago, when there were only 13 states. Each state had its own government, as they do today. But the states were so loosely united that they acted like separate little countries. Many leaders wanted to make the union of the states stronger. These leaders planned a meeting in Philadelphia to discuss how to improve their national government. They asked all the states to choose men to come to the meeting.

The meeting was called the Constitutional Convention. It began on May 25, 1787, and continued through the summer. Fifty-seven men helped write a new document joining the states together—the Constitution. On September 17, 39 of the men signed it. The original, written out by hand, is on display in the National Archives Building in Washington, D.C.

The men who signed the Constitution are sometimes called the Founding Fathers because they did so much to found—set up—the government of the United States. One of the men, George Washington, had commanded the colonial army that fought the British in the Revolutionary War. Benjamin Franklin, 81 years old, helped keep order when the men argued about the new government. James Madison, sometimes called the "father of the Constitution," helped the men agree on what the Constitution should say. He also kept a record of the meetings at the convention. Gouverneur Morris helped write the final draft.

Before the Constitution could become law, 9 of the 13 states had to ratify it—approve it. Delaware was the first state to do so. New Hampshire was the ninth. In June 1788, the Constitution went into effect. Six months later, George Washington was elected the first president of the United States. Like every president since then, he promised to "preserve, protect, and defend the Constitution of the United States." In 1790, Rhode Island became the last of the 13 original states to join the United States.

The Constitution has three parts. The first part, the Preamble, is an introduction. It begins with the words "We the people." This makes it clear that the people—not a king or dictator—are in charge. In other words, the Constitution outlines a *democratic* form of government.

The main part of the Constitution is next. It has seven sections, called *articles,* telling how the government will work. These articles give some powers to the national government and others to the states.

Article I is about Congress, the branch of the government that can make new laws. This article explains how people will be chosen for Congress and what powers Congress will have. It gives Congress the power to make tax laws so the government can raise money. (*See* **Congress, United States.**)

Article II concerns the president and the vice president, who are in charge of carrying out the laws passed by Congress. (*See* **presidents of the United States.**)

Article III is about the national law courts, which must make sure that the laws are fair. The most important is the Supreme Court. (*See* **Supreme Court, United States.**)

Article IV describes how the states cooperate with each other and with the national government.

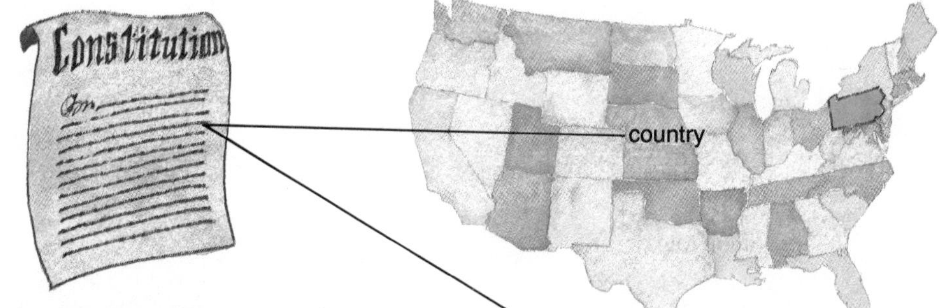

The Constitution outlines a *federal* system in which power is shared by national, state, and local governments.

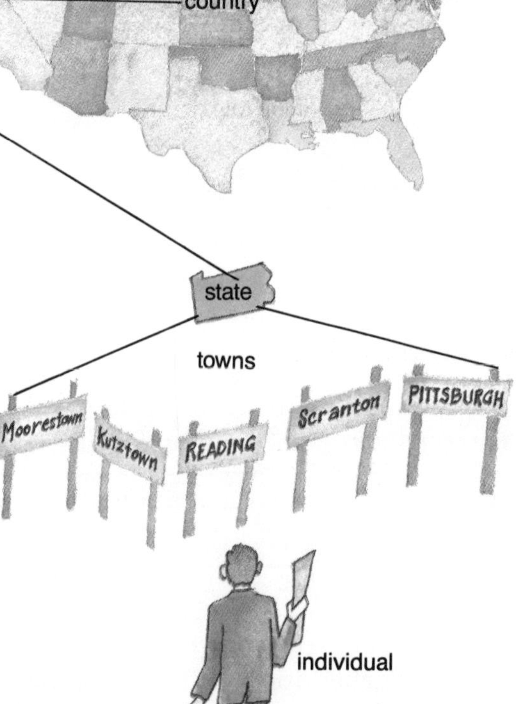

Local governments—towns or counties—are responsible for running public schools.

Article V describes how the Constitution can be changed. This is done by making additions to the Constitution, which are called *amendments*.

Article VI says that the Constitution is "the supreme law of the land." If state laws disagree with it, they must be changed.

Article VII describes how the states should ratify the Constitution.

The amendments make up the third part of the Constitution. There have been 26 of these changes since 1788. The first ten amendments are called the Bill of Rights. They were made all at once, three and a half years after the Constitution became law. These ten amendments protect the basic rights of all Americans, including freedom of religion, freedom of speech, and freedom of the press. (*See* **Bill of Rights.**)

There have been other important amendments. After the Civil War, Amendments 13, 14, and 15 ended slavery and gave black people all the rights of citizenship. Before 1920, only men could vote in national elections. Amendment 19 gave women the right to vote. Before 1971, people had to be 21 years old to vote. Amendment 26 lowered the voting age to 18.

In 1987, the Constitution was 200 years old. Over those two centuries, the country has grown from 13 states and 4 million people to 50 states and 250 million people. Life is different in many ways. But the Constitution, written by the Founding Fathers so long ago, is still the basis of the democratic government of the United States.

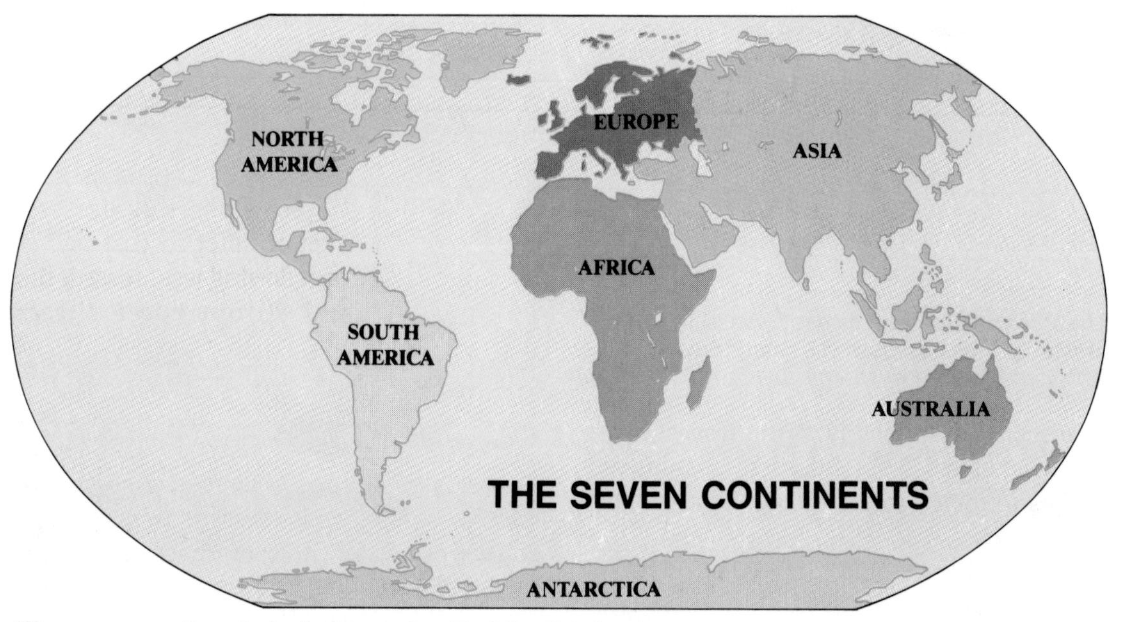

The seven continents include nearly all of Earth's land area.

continent

The earth has seven large areas of land, called continents. Together, the seven continents make up about one third of the earth's surface. The rest is under the oceans.

In order of size, the continents are Asia, Africa, North America, South America, Antarctica, Europe, and Australia. Continents formed early in the history of the earth. They were not exactly the same as today's continents. (*See* **continental drift.**)

The seven continents are not all separated. In fact, only Australia and Antarctica are fully separated from the others by oceans. North and South America are joined by a narrow strip of land. Africa touches Asia. Europe and Asia share such a long border that they are sometimes thought of as a single continent, Eurasia.

Long ago, when the earth's crust—outer skin—first began forming, it separated into two kinds of rock. One kind was lighter than the other, both in weight and in color. It became the *continental crust*—the foundation for the continents. This kind of rock is made mostly of the element aluminum plus a combination of silicon and oxygen called *silica.* The most common of these rocks is called *granite.* The heavier, darker kind of rock forms the *oceanic crust*—the floor of the earth's oceans. It contains iron and magnesium as well as silica. The most common of these rocks is called *basalt.*

When the two kinds of rock began to separate, the continental crust gradually rose up through the oceanic crust because it was lighter. This happened during the first billion years of the earth's history. With time, the continental crust began to form a separate layer on top of the oceanic crust, like icing on a cake.

Oceanic crust is about 6 kilometers (4 miles) thick. Continental crust is much thicker—about 35 kilometers (22 miles). Beneath mountains and plateaus, continental crust can be as thick as 70 kilometers (40 miles). That is more than 10 times as thick as oceanic crust.

Oceanic crust lies far below sea level, while most of the continental crust is above the sea. The land we live on is continental crust.

The small part of the continental crust that is below sea level is called the *continental shelf.* Each continent's shelf lies under the shallow waters of the oceans near land.

The continental shelf slopes gradually downward as it extends out from the shore. At its deepest point, the shelf lies more than 200 meters (600 feet) under the sea.

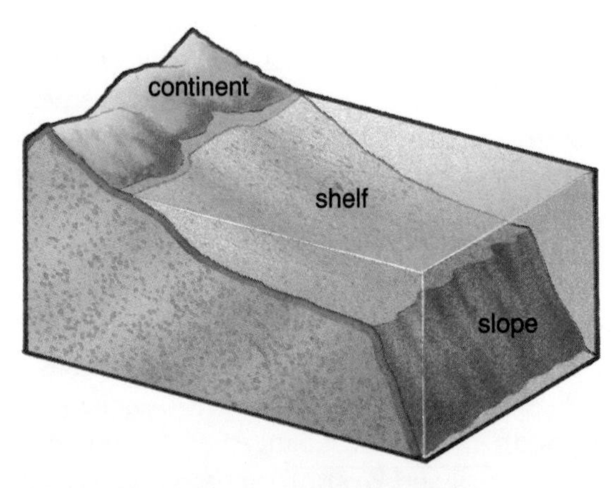

The water above a continental shelf is home to many living things.

The width of a continental shelf is very different from one place to another. Off the Atlantic coast of South America, the shelf is 560 kilometers (350 miles) wide and extends out as far as the Falkland Islands. Off the Pacific coast of South America, the shelf is only about 200 kilometers (124 miles) wide.

Some of the world's largest islands stand on a continental shelf. We consider such an island part of the continent from which that shelf extends. The islands of Great Britain and Ireland rise from the continental shelf of Europe and are part of that continent. Greenland is part of North America.

Beyond a continental shelf, the bottom of the sea slopes steeply downward. This downhill region is the *continental slope.* It descends to broad, level plains that lie beneath 5 kilometers (3 miles) of seawater.

The continental shelf is an important source of natural resources. The Grand Banks off the Atlantic coast of Canada is one of the world's richest fishing grounds. It is part of North America's continental shelf. Other important resources found in shelf areas are oil and gas.

See also **earth history; island; geology;** and **rock.**

continental divide

If you cross the Rocky Mountains by road, you will come to a sign that says "Continental Divide." We also call the Continental Divide the Great Divide. Along this line you could pour a bucket of water so that half of it runs into a stream flowing west toward the Pacific. The other half runs into a stream flowing east toward the Gulf of Mexico, an arm of the Atlantic.

A divide is an imaginary line on the earth's surface. All the streams on one side of a divide empty into one body of water. All the streams on the other side empty into a different body of water. All continents have continental divides.

In northern Canada and Alaska, the divide runs through the Rockies and other high mountains. The waters east of the divide flow into Hudson Bay and the Arctic Ocean.

South of the United States, in Mexico and Central America, the continental divide follows a line of mountain peaks and high plateaus. Waters on the west side flow into the Pacific. Waters to the east flow into the Caribbean Sea. In South America, the continental divide follows the western Andes.

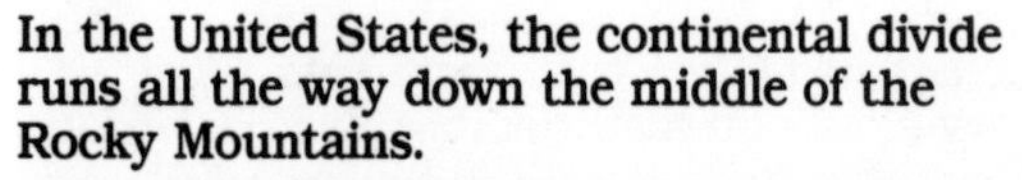

In the United States, the continental divide runs all the way down the middle of the Rocky Mountains.

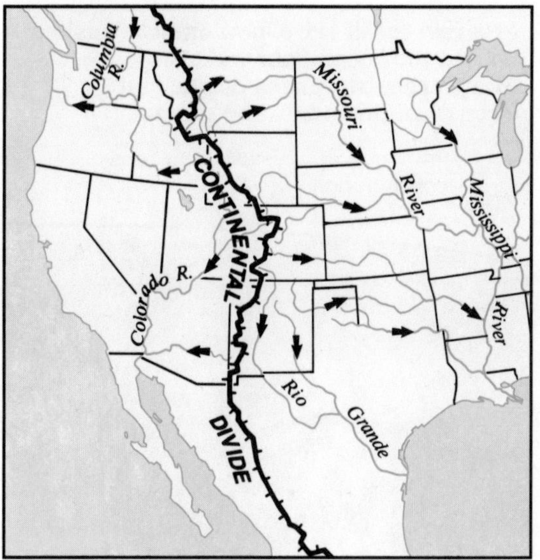

continental drift

If you look at a map of the Atlantic Ocean, you can see that Africa and South America look like two matching pieces of a jigsaw puzzle. The bulge of Brazil would fit neatly into Africa's Gulf of Guinea. Is it possible that the two continents once did fit together? Scientists think so. Long ago, the continents may have been one huge land. The theory that explains how the continents have moved apart is called continental drift.

The theory of continental drift was proposed in 1912 by a German scientist named Alfred Wegener. He showed how the coasts of South America and Africa looked as though they could fit together. He reported that Brazil and West Africa have many of the same kinds of rocks and minerals. Wegener also found fossil remains of the same kinds of ancient plants and animals in both places.

Wegener said that in the past, all seven continents were joined together. They formed one giant land that he called Pangaea. About 200 million years ago, Pangaea broke into two parts, Wegener said. He called the two Laurasia and Gondwanaland. From these two landmasses, all seven of today's continents formed. He said the continents floated on the floor of the oceans.

Wegener's theory was not accepted. Other scientists argued that continents could not move on the ocean floor. They said there

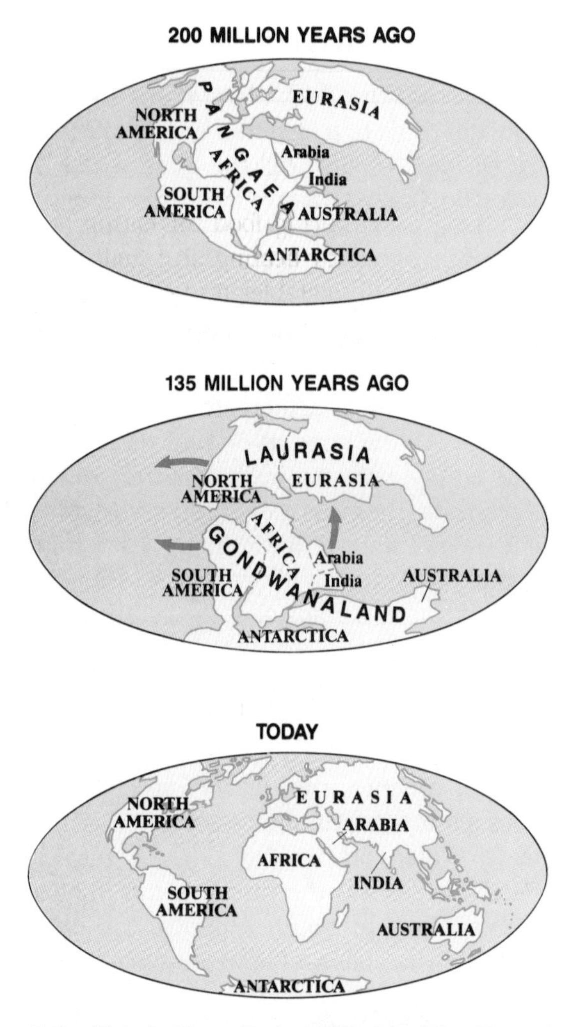

Scientists believe that continents "float" very slowly on plates across Earth's surface.

At a mid ocean ridge, new crust is pushed up and the ocean floor widens.
At a trench, two plates collide and force crust down into the magma.

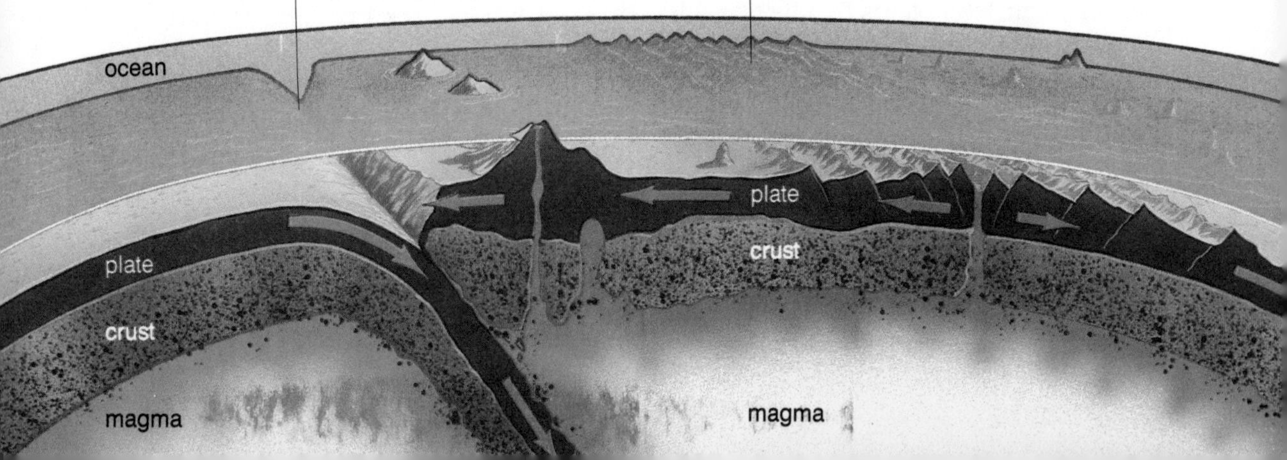

must be other explanations for the similar coastlines, minerals, and fossils.

Then, in the early 1960s, scientists studying the ocean floor made a surprising discovery. Hot rock rising through a long crack was creating new ocean floor in the middle of the Atlantic. In order to make room for the new seafloor, the rocks on opposite sides of the middle were moving away from each other. So, while the eastern part of the floor of the Atlantic was moving toward Europe and Africa, the western part was moving toward North and South America.

Eventually, they discovered that not only was the seafloor spreading, it was carrying the continents with it. This meant that Africa and South America were drifting away from each other very slowly. Each year, the Atlantic Ocean gets about 1 inch (2.5 centimeters) wider; and Africa and South America are about 1 inch farther apart.

Today, many scientists accept Wegener's theory of continental drift. They have discovered that continents really can move over the surface of the earth. Scientists now see that the earth's crust—its outer surface—is not one unbroken shell. It is divided into about 20 great pieces, called *plates.* Some of these plates are made of ocean floor. Some are made of both ocean floor and continents. All the plates are moving. The study of the ways they move is called *plate tectonics.*

Since the discovery that the ocean floor is spreading, there have been other discoveries. If new crust was being created beneath the seas, wouldn't old crust have to be destroyed somewhere else? Otherwise, the earth's crust would grow too large for the planet and begin to look like a big, baggy jacket.

Where was the old crust being destroyed? Again, the seafloor held the answer. Just as it spreads apart in some places, it plunges into the earth in other places, forming long, deep trenches. The bottom of one such trench, in the Pacific Ocean, is almost 12 kilometers (7 miles) below sea level!

See also **continent; earth history; volcano;** and **earthquake.**

Cook, Captain James, *see* explorers

cooking

Cooking is preparing food for eating. Most cooking is done by heating. But making salads from raw vegetables and making sandwiches without heating are also considered cooking.

A food may be cooked by itself, without adding anything. Some people take a piece of meat or an unpeeled potato and just heat it. Most food, however, is combined with spices, herbs, or other foods. People often add salt or a liquid such as milk, broth, or water to a food before or during cooking. All of the foods used in preparing a dish are called *ingredients.* The ingredients of a peanut butter and jelly sandwich are 2 slices of bread, 2 tablespoons of peanut butter, and 1 tablespoon of jelly.

Cooking is preparing food—including cleaning it, heating it, and freezing it.

A *recipe* is a list of ingredients with directions telling what to do with them. Many cooks follow recipes to prepare food. When a recipe says "1 cup," it does not mean just any cup. It means 1 measuring cup, which holds 8 ounces. There are also special measuring spoons. Some cooks measure ingredients by weight. Either way, many cooks use the metric system. They measure everything in parts of liters and grams.

Cooking Methods The first cooking was probably done over an open fire. Then people invented pots and ovens. Some people found they could heat liquid by dropping hot stones into it. Others cooked on a hot, flat stone. For thousands of years, wood was the main cooking fuel in most places. Now we have stoves that use gas and electricity. In some parts of the world, people still use old methods.

WAYS TO COOK FOOD

There are many methods of cooking in a modern kitchen. Here are the best-known.

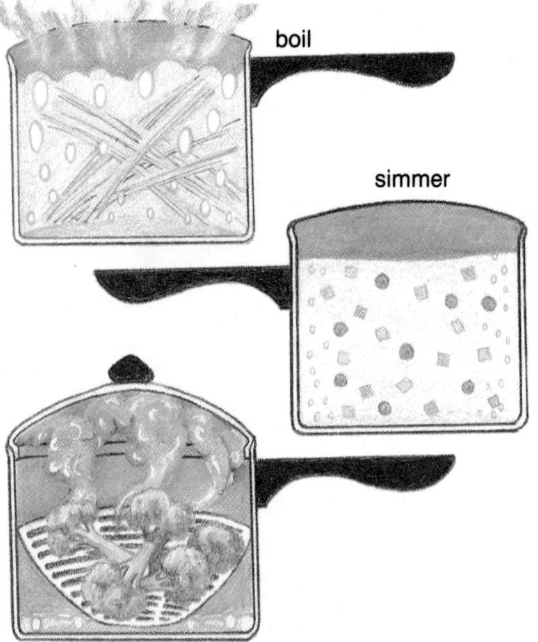

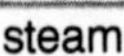

Boiling is done in bubbling hot water or another liquid. Almost any food can be boiled — potatoes, rice, eggs, and so on.

Simmering is cooking in liquid that is not boiling hot. When liquid simmers, there are only tiny bubbles around the edge, not big bubbles all through.

Steaming cooks food in the hot steam made by a boiling liquid, usually water. Some foods are placed above, not in, the boiling liquid. Others are steamed in a small amount of liquid.

Braising is done in two steps. First the meat or vegetable is browned quickly over high heat. Then the food is cooked slowly in liquid in a covered pot.

Broiling cooks food right under or over heat without adding fat or liquid. Broiling is often used for meat, fish, and poultry.

Frying cooks food in hot fat or oil. Deep-frying is done in a deep pot with enough oil to cover the food. Pan-frying cooks the food in a frying pan in a small amount of fat or oil. *Sautéing* is another word for pan-frying. Stir-frying cooks food very quickly in a small amount of oil or fat. Foods to be stir-fried are first cut into small pieces so they will cook fast.

Pan-broiling is cooking in a heavy frying pan without fat. Any fat that comes from the food as it cooks is removed. Otherwise, the food will be fried, not broiled.

People in different parts of the world often like particular combinations of ingredients and ways of cooking them. In America, broiled cheeseburgers and french fries are popular. In Italy, pasta is served often, with a variety of sauces. In China, vegetables and meat are often stir-fried and served together. In most of Asia, rice is a part of almost every meal.

See also **food** and **eating customs.**

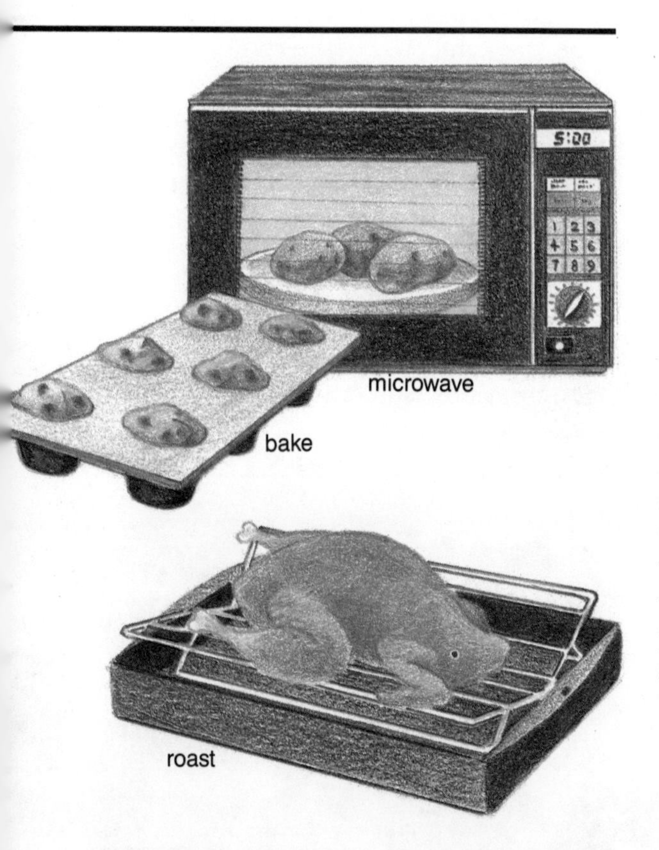

Baking cooks the food in a closed oven. The food usually is not covered. Breads, cakes, and cookies are baked. So are apples, potatoes, and other vegetables and fruit.

Roasting done in an oven is the same as baking. Some kinds of meat, such as beef and lamb, are roasted in the oven. Roasting can also be done over an open fire.

Microwave cooking is a fairly new method of preparing food. A special microwave oven is used. The food cooks more quickly than it does in a regular oven.

Coolidge, Calvin, *see* presidents of the U.S.

Copernicus, Nicolaus

Nicolaus Copernicus was a Polish astronomer who was the first to convince people that Earth and other planets revolve around the sun. He is often called the "founder of modern astronomy."

At the time when Copernicus lived—1473 to 1543—astronomers thought Earth was standing still at the center of the universe. They thought the sun and other planets revolved around Earth. The ancient Greeks developed this idea to explain what they saw in the sky—the sun rising and setting, the phases of the moon, and the planets appearing at different places in the sky. People believed this for almost 2,000 years.

Copernicus was not the first astronomer to find that something was wrong with the Greek system. But he was the first to describe our solar system correctly. He said the sun was at the center of the solar system, and that the planets were traveling around the sun. Mercury, Venus, Earth, Mars, Jupiter, and Saturn were the only planets known then. But Copernicus showed them in their proper order around the sun. He also showed that the moon orbited Earth.

See also **astronomy** and **solar system.**

copper

Copper is a soft, reddish-orange metal. If your hot and cold water pipes are reddish, then they are made from copper. Most of the electrical wiring in buildings, telephones, TV sets, tape recorders, and radios is also made from copper. Even our bodies contain small amounts of copper, which helps to make the coloring pigments for our skins.

People have used copper for over 5,000 years. In the earth, it is usually combined with other elements. Our ancestors used hot fires to release the copper from these other substances. Today, copper is taken from mines all over the world.

Next to silver, copper is the best conductor of electricity. Copper is 15 percent lighter than silver, and its melting point is higher. It costs 90 percent less. For these reasons, 50 percent of the copper produced each year is used in electrical generators, transformers, and motors, or for wiring in computers, appliances, and electronic equipment.

Copper also conducts heat very well and stands up to high temperatures. That is why many pots and pans are made from copper, or have copper bottoms. The copper spreads heat well, so food cooks evenly. Shiny copper pans and other copper objects are also prized for their beauty.

See also **alloy.**

coral

Corals are very tiny animals that live in seas. Even though small in size, they build some of the biggest structures on earth. They build coral reefs and coral islands. The most famous coral reef is the Great Barrier Reef off the northeast coast of Australia. It is 2,000 kilometers (1,250 miles) long. (*See* **Australia** and **reef.**)

Corals are related to jellyfish and sea anemones. A coral has a hollow body shaped like a tube. An opening at one end is the mouth. Around the mouth are fingerlike tentacles armed with stinging cells. The coral's tentacles catch small animals and push them into its mouth.

Each coral grows a hard skeleton shaped like a cup outside its body. The skeleton protects the coral. When the coral dies, other corals build their own skeletons on top of the empty cup. Gradually, a large mass forms. The mass may consist of billions and billions of coral skeletons. There are living animals only on the outside.

Most corals live in warm, shallow waters, in large groups called *colonies.* Coral colonies have different shapes. Some, like brain coral, are round. Others, like staghorn coral, have branches. Still others look like fans or mushrooms or lace.

Corals have many sizes and shapes. Below, a colorful group of corals provides a hiding place for a fish. Most corals live where the sea is warm and shallow.

corn

Along with wheat, rice, and potatoes, corn is one of the four major crops in the world. Corn is the most widely produced grain in the United States. But the sweet corn that we eat is only a small portion of the corn grown each year. Most of the corn grown in the United States is used to feed livestock and to produce many other foods, such as corn oil, cornstarch, and corn syrup.

You may have seen corn growing in a field. Crowning the top of each tall plant is a golden *tassel*. This is the male structure of the plant and contains pollen. At the end of each young ear of corn is *corn silk*—a female structure. Wind blows pollen from the tassel to the silk. The pollen travels down the strands of silk and pollinates the egg at the bottom of each one. A seed or kernel begins to grow from each egg.

The ear of corn that we eat contains hundreds of kernels—the seeds for the next generation of plants. If the corn were left alone, the ears would fall to the ground. The next generation of plants would be so close together that only a few would survive. So corn must be *cultivated*—grown by people. It cannot survive without our help.

Corn came from a wild grass similar to that of other grains. People started growing corn thousands of years ago in both North and South America. In some caves in Mexico, scientists have found corncobs smaller than your little finger. They may be 5,000 years old. Corn was grown by the Inca of Peru, the Aztec of Mexico, and the Maya of Guatemala. They always took some seeds from the plants with the largest and tastiest ears to plant the next year. After many many years, the ears of corn were larger.

When Columbus and other Europeans came to the New World, they saw corn for the first time. American Indians called the grain *maize*. They ground it into flour and baked it into loaves of bread. European settlers were introduced to maize by the Indians and soon began cultivating it, too.

Today, corn is grown all over the United States, but especially in the fertile soil of the "corn belt" states—Iowa, Illinois, and Indiana. It is also grown in many other countries around the world.

See also **farming**; **grain**; and **hybrid seed**.

Some corn plants produce only one ear of corn. Others may have as many as eight.

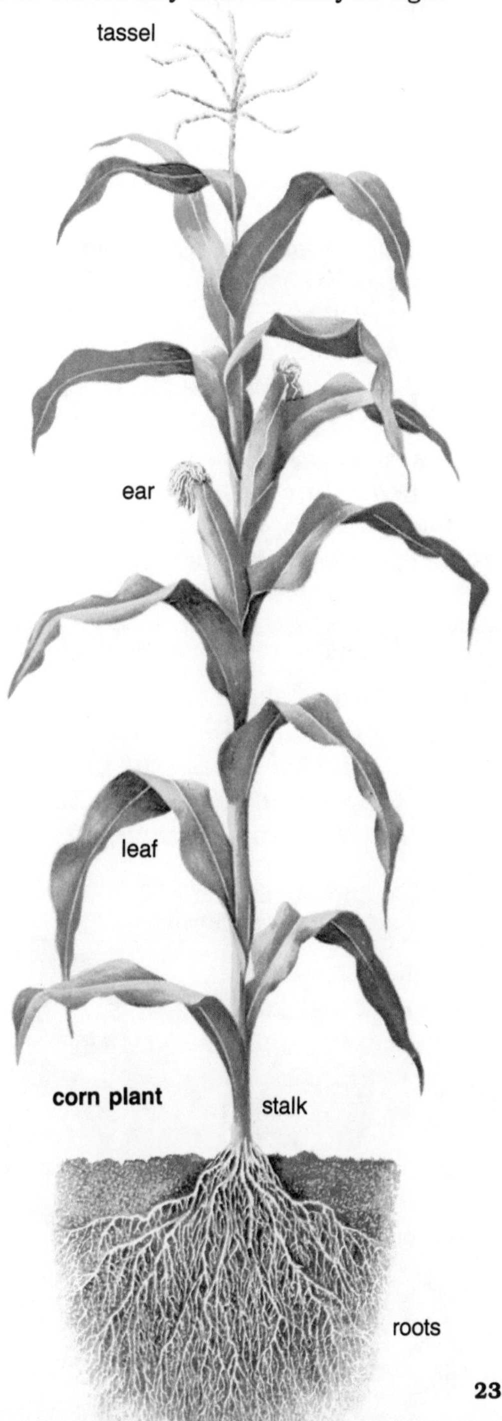

Coronado, Francisco, *see* explorers

Cortés, Hernando

In the early 1500s, a small force of Spanish soldiers conquered the vast empire of the Aztec in Mexico. They were led by a daring captain named Hernando Cortés.

Cortés came to America seeking wealth and adventure. He tried farming on an island in the Caribbean, then joined in the invasion of Cuba. Then he heard about the riches of the Aztec. In 1519, Cortés invaded Mexico with about 500 soldiers. On the march to the Aztec capital, he gained many Indian allies. They hated Aztec rule and admired the Spaniards' horses and guns.

The Aztec ruler, Montezuma, thought Cortés might be a god. Aztec legends said one of their great gods had disappeared but would someday return. When the Spaniards reached the Aztec capital, they put Montezuma in prison. When the Aztec finally did attack, the Spanish and their Indian allies defeated them. Montezuma was killed. Cortés soon controlled all of Central Mexico.

Cortés later explored in Central America and Lower California. He became the richest person in Spanish America. In 1540, he returned to Spain, where he died in 1547.

See also **Aztec** and **Montezuma.**

Hernando Cortés, conqueror of the Aztec empire in Mexico.

Cosmetics range from makeup and perfume to hair tonic, after-shave lotion, and toothpaste.

cosmetics

Cosmetics are preparations used on the body to make a person more attractive. Shampoo, toothpaste, makeup, nail polish, perfume, and deodorants are all cosmetics. Soap is not considered a cosmetic. In the United States, Canada, and several other countries, the government has rules to be sure that cosmetics are safe to use.

One way to group cosmetics is by what they do. One group is *makeup.* Makeup adds color to the face or body. In the United States, most makeup is used on the face. Face powder, lipstick, eye shadow, mascara, and rouge are kinds of face makeup. In some places, people use makeup on their bodies as well. Actors use special makeup to make them look right for the parts they play. Actors' makeup helps change their appearance. At a fair you may have your face made up just for fun. Makeup can also be part of a costume at a costume party.

Another group of cosmetics includes perfumes, colognes, and other scented products. People use these to make themselves smell good. Perfume is stronger and lasts longer than cologne.

Skin-care products are another group of cosmetics. Some clean the skin. Others keep

the skin from becoming dry. Some—such as cold cream—do both. There are even creams and lotions that can help smooth out wrinkles, if they are used every day.

Cosmetics for the hair include shampoos, rinses, dyes, bleaches, and products to make a hairdo keep its shape. Cosmetics for the nails include nail polish and fake nails.

Cosmetics have been used for most of human history, in all parts of the world. One of the best-known ancient cosmetics was an eye makeup called *kohl.* When you look at ancient Egyptian paintings, you can see the dark kohl around people's eyes. It is still used in some parts of the world.

About 5,000 substances are used in manufacturing cosmetics. Oil, wax, alcohol, talc, and dyes are common ingredients. Some people are allergic to certain ingredients in cosmetics. There are special cosmetics for these people.

Men and women usually use different kinds of cosmetics. Men use hair creams, after-shave lotions, skin conditioners, and hand creams. In the United States, women are more likely than men to use everyday makeup. People use cosmetics because they feel better when they know they look and smell good.

See also **perfume.**

cosmic ray

When radioactivity was first discovered, the scientist Victor Hess thought he could show that the earth itself was slightly radioactive. He went up in balloons to measure radioactivity away from the earth. He expected that there wouldn't be any so high in the sky. Instead, he found eight times as much radioactivity as there was at the earth's surface. This is how Hess discovered cosmic rays. (*See* **radioactivity.**)

Cosmic rays are fast-moving pieces of atoms that come from outer space. The pieces that crash into the earth's outer atmosphere are usually the larger ones. These are called *primary cosmic rays.* When the primary cosmic rays hit atoms in the air, they send out smaller fragments. These are called *secondary cosmic rays.* Many secondary cosmic rays are strange particles that do not come from ordinary matter. Scientists have learned much about the universe by studying these unusual particles.

This huge supernova, which appeared in 1987, is one of many stars that shower Earth with cosmic rays.

The sun and other nearby stars send out some of the cosmic rays that bombard Earth. But astronomers believe most cosmic rays are produced by *supernovae*—stars exploding way out in deep space. (*See* **star.**)

Costa Rica, *see* Central America

cotton

Cotton is a plant that produces a very important fiber. Cotton is also the name of the fiber, of the thread made from the fiber, and of the cloth made from that thread.

The cotton plant grows in warm climates. The plant first produces flowers. They drop off quickly, each flower leaving a *boll.* The cotton boll contains the seeds and the fibers. When the cotton bolls are ripe, they split open and look white and fluffy. They are ready to be picked.

While cotton is growing, it needs a lot of care. Weeds must be removed and the plants must be protected from diseases and insects. An insect, the boll weevil, can ruin a cotton crop. Weevils may cost cotton farmers thousands of dollars.

After the cotton bolls are picked, the seeds must be removed from the fibers. This job is done by a cotton gin, a machine invented by Eli Whitney in 1793. (*See* **Whitney, Eli.**)

The cotton fibers then go through several stages to turn them into thread. Some of the thread will remain thread, used for sewing. But most of the thread will be woven or knitted into cloth for clothing and other needs. T-shirts and underwear are two products made from cotton knit.

The cottonseed used to be thrown away, but now many products are made from it. Cottonseed oil, pressed out of the seeds, is used for cooking and cosmetics. Part of the seed is used for cattle feed, fertilizer, and fuel. The fuzz on the outside of the seed is used for making cotton balls.

The United States is one of the major cotton-growing countries. Many of the southern states grow cotton and also make cotton thread and cloth. For a while, it seemed that synthetic fibers such as nylon, made from chemicals, would replace cotton. But today, much cloth is made from a mixture of cotton and synthetic threads. Cotton makes the cloth more comfortable and more absorbent. The synthetic threads make it stronger and easier to take care of. (*See* **synthetic fabric.**)

Cotton has played an important part in the history of the United States. Before the Civil War, owners of large cotton plantations in the South used slaves to do the hard work in the fields. The system of slavery was one of the causes of the Civil War. Now, most cotton-growing work is done by machines.

See also **clothmaking.**

We make thread and cloth from cotton plants, and a cooking oil from their seeds.

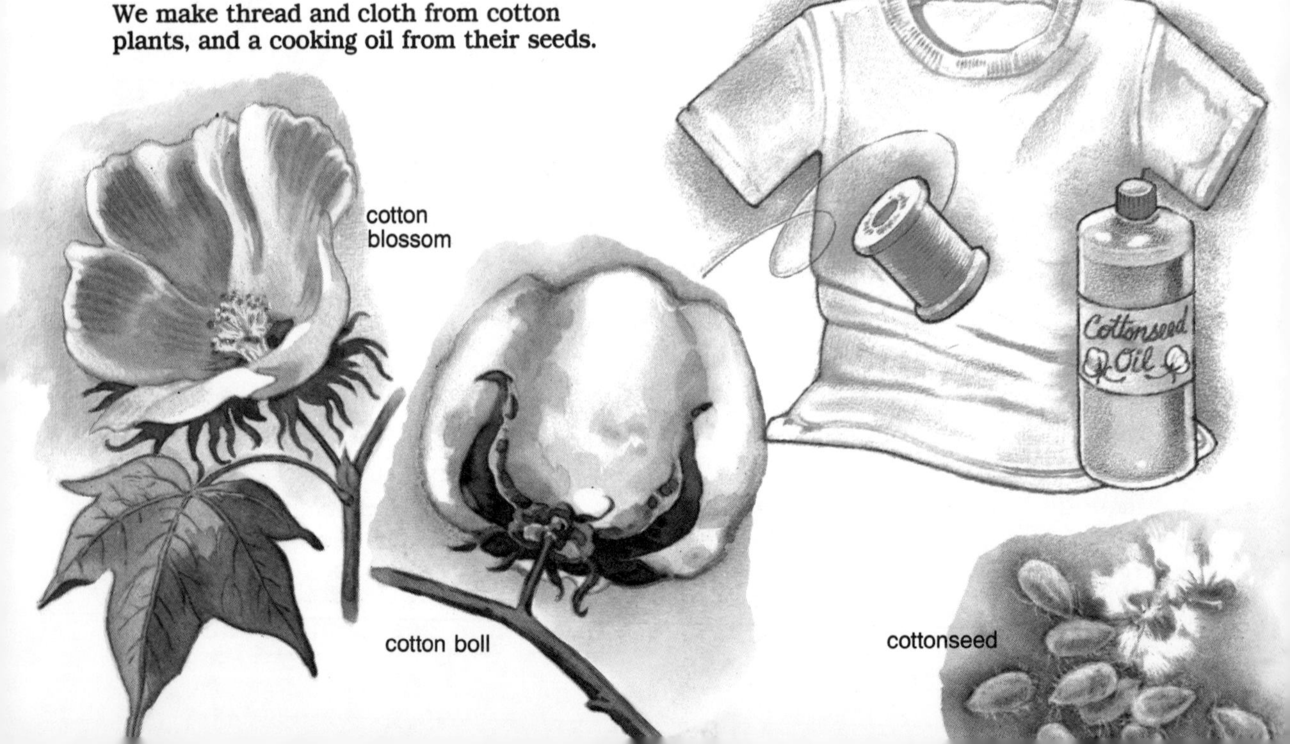

country

Sometimes we use the word *country* to mean the opposite of *city*. The word makes us think of open spaces and farms. Usually, however, *country* means the same as *nation* —a territory with definite boundaries and its own government. A country is independent—it does not belong to any other nation. It usually has its own flag. It also has a capital city, where the government has its headquarters. For instance, the capital of the United States is Washington, D.C. The capital of France is Paris.

Each country has its own flag and issues its own money, stamps, and passports.

There are about 170 countries in the world today. The largest is the Soviet Union, also known as Russia. It has over 8 million square miles (20 million square kilometers). About a fourth of this land lies on the continent of Europe. The rest is in Asia. This is unusual, for most countries are located on a single continent.

The world's smallest country is Monaco, in Europe. It is less than 1 square mile in size. This tiny country, almost surrounded by France, consists of three towns along the Mediterranean Sea.

Another unusual country is the Vatican. It is located in the city of Rome and is the headquarters of the Roman Catholic church.

Some countries are very old. Egypt, in northern Africa, had its beginnings about 4000 B.C.—almost 6,000 years ago. Other countries are quite new. For example, Vanuatu became a country in 1980. It is made up of several islands in the Pacific Ocean, east of Australia.

Countries are formed in many different ways. A new country can begin when a territory that once belonged to another country gains its independence. This is how the United States became a country. It used to be 13 different colonies that belonged to England. (*See* **colony.**)

Countries may also be formed when a single country splits into two or more parts. At the time of World War II, Germany was one country. After the war, it split into two nations—West Germany and East Germany.

Still another way of forming a country is when several separate countries join together. In the early 1900s, there were many small nations in southeastern Europe. Today they are one country, called Yugoslavia.

See the index for entries on individual countries.

country music

Country music is a kind of music that began in the southern Appalachian mountains of the United States. Country singers often sing alone and accompany themselves on guitar. Today, country groups may also use electric guitars, banjos, harmonicas, and many other instruments.

The most important country-music program, the "Grand Ole Opry," has been broadcast from Nashville, Tennessee, since 1924. Each year, thousands of country-music fans visit Opryland, near Nashville, to see the show.

Western music is much like country music, but it tells about lonely cowboys and others in the huge wilderness of the West. Country and western songs are often sad songs about losing someone you love. Other songs are about the lives of mountain people. They tell about working in Appalachian coal mines or on the railroads. Some country songs express religious feelings.

A young fiddler joins other musicians at a country-music gathering in Tennessee.

Cowboys lived on the range for months. Their food was cooked in chuck wagons. Top, Deadwood Dick, a famous black cowboy. Far right, modern cowboys bring hay in trucks to feed cattle during a blizzard.

Country music is most popular in the southern and western United States. It has many fans in other regions as well. Country and western stars, such as Willie Nelson and Loretta Lynn, often appear in live concerts and on television.

cow, *see* cattle; dairying

cowboy

The old-time American cowboy was a tough, hard-riding man. One of his main jobs was to round up cattle and move them across the untamed American West.

The first cowboys were Indians trained to work for wealthy ranchers in Mexico and California. The Spanish called them *vaqueros.* Later, many cowboys were blacks.

By 1860, more than 3 million cattle—"longhorns"—roamed the plains of Texas. After the Civil War, when beef was scarce in the East, people looked to Texas to supply the nation with beef.

Cowboys on horseback rounded up the longhorns into large groups, then went on long *cattle drives,* herding the cattle north. Towns like Abilene, Kansas, sprang up where the trail met the railroad that would take the cattle east.

Life on the trail was hard. The men slept on the ground. Before dawn, they would roll out of their blankets and have breakfast. Then they would saddle their horses and ride alongside the herd, chasing back any cattle that strayed. They tried to keep the cattle from becoming frightened and *stampeding*—running wild. The herd had to walk 25 or 30 miles (40 to 48 kilometers) each day. The cowboys might be on their horses for 18 hours at a time.

In the evening, the cowboys would coax their cattle—including motherless calves called *dogies*—to lie down and sleep. Some cowboys sang songs or told stories around the campfire. Others took night watch.

During the fall and spring roundups, cattle on the open range were herded together. Not all the cattle belonged to one owner. Cowboys working for each owner had to separate their own cattle from the large herd. Cowboys used their *lariats* or *lassos* to rope the cattle. They branded new calves with a hot iron bearing the symbol of the owner. Branding was meant to prevent disputes about who owned the cattle. Yet cattle stealing—*rustling*—was common.

Later, when barbed wire was invented, the open range was fenced along property lines. The railroad soon reached Texas, so long cattle drives were no longer necessary.

Cowhands on ranches today—men and women—have trucks and machinery to help them with their work. Many are still fine riders. They often exhibit their riding and roping skills in rodeos.

See also **ranch** and **rodeo.**

Coyotes live in Canada, the United States, Mexico, and parts of Central America.

coyote

The coyote is a wild dog. It looks very much like a wolf but is smaller. Most coyotes weigh about 13 kilograms (29 pounds), roughly the same as a cocker spaniel.

Coyotes are found throughout North America, in grasslands and other open country. In the United States, coyotes used to live only in the West. Recently, they have spread to the East.

Unlike wolves, coyotes rarely run in packs. They hunt alone or in family groups, seeking many different foods. They eat insects, mice, and other small animals. They also eat dead animals, garbage, and fruits.

Scientists believe that coyotes mate for life. They are excellent parents. They take turns feeding the pups. Later, they teach the pups how to catch their own prey.

Coyotes are shy, so they avoid people. Though they are seldom seen, coyotes can often be heard. At sunrise and sunset, they "sing"—howl, bark, and yap, often in a chorus. No other animal sings such a song.

See also **dog family.**

CPR, *see* first aid

crab

Crabs are relatives of shrimps, lobsters, and barnacles. They belong to a group of animals called *crustaceans.* Like other crustaceans, the crab has a shell. The shell is made of many pieces joined together by thin, soft sections. The soft sections let the crab move. (*See* **crustacean.**)

Many crabs have a funny walk. Instead of moving forward, they move sideways or at an angle. A crab has five pairs of walking legs. The front pair are usually much bigger than the others and have large claws for fighting and for catching food.

Some crabs live in fresh water or in wet places on land. But most crabs live in the sea. Some live among rocks near the shore. Others burrow into sand and mud on the seafloor. People like to eat crabs, and crabbing—catching crabs—is an important business in many parts of the world.

Blue crabs are found in the waters off the east coast of the United States.

There are more than 4,000 known kinds of crabs. The shell of the smallest kind is only 6 millimeters (¼-inch) across. The largest has a shell more than 30 centimeters (12 inches) wide. Some crabs have enormous legs. When the legs of a giant Japanese spider crab are spread out, the animal may be nearly 3 meters (9 feet) across!

cranes and derricks

Cranes and derricks are machines that have a long arm, called a *boom,* for lifting and moving heavy loads. Most cranes can travel from one place to another on their own power. Derricks usually stay in one place and move only their booms.

Different kinds of cranes do different jobs. A tow truck for automobiles has a small crane mounted at the rear. Larger cranes are used in road construction. These cranes are mounted on truck wheels or tractor treads. Cranes may also sit on railroad cars or barges.

A crane's boom reaches out from a heavy base that keeps a crane from tipping over. At the end of the boom is a pulley. A strong cable is anchored to the base and passes through the pulley. There is a reel to wind up the cable.

Different tools can be hung from the end of the cable to do different jobs. A hook, a sling, or a set of big steel jaws may be used for picking up heavy objects and moving them. A bucket may be used for digging. To knock down buildings, a crane swings a big steel wrecking ball. In junkyards, an electric magnet attached to the cable lifts steel and iron.

A crane operator works the controls in the cab on the crane's base. A powerful engine winds and unwinds the cable. Other controls can swing the boom in a circle.

Some cranes travel only in limited ways. A bridge crane is one example. It has a bridge that crosses over the work area. Only the lifting machinery and sometimes the cab travel back and forth along the bridge. But the bridge itself can move. The bridge is on tracks, like a railroad car. It can carry the cab and the lifting machinery to different parts of the work area. Bridge cranes are used to transport molten metal in foundries. They are also used in shipyards to transfer coal and other cargo. Bridge cranes are used at NASA space centers, too.

Although derricks stay in one place, they do many jobs. Oil derricks raise and lower drilling equipment used to find oil. On freighters, derricks handle cargo. Some derricks can be taken apart and set up in different places.

Derricks have a tall *mast*—pole—that is anchored to the ground. The mast supports the boom, which is hinged near the bottom of the mast. Like a crane, a derrick has a pulley located at the far end of the boom. But a derrick's controls are often located in a nearby shed instead of in a cab.

A crane about eight stories tall lifts materials to the top of a new building.

If a crayfish loses a leg or claw, a new one will grow back in its place.

crayfish

A crayfish looks like a small lobster. It has the same shape and large claws on its two front legs for fighting and for catching food. But lobsters live in the sea, and crayfish live in fresh water. Crayfish live in lakes, ponds, and streams. Some live in burrows in swamps and wet meadows. They live on every continent except Africa and Antarctica.

Crayfish belong to a group of animals called *crustaceans.* Like all crustaceans, crayfish have a shell made of many pieces. (*See* **crustacean.**)

Usually, crayfish crawl forward on four pairs of walking legs. But if danger approaches, a crayfish will quickly swim backward to get away. It does this by rapidly flicking the back end of its body.

Crayfish do not like heat. They usually spend the day under rocks or in burrows. They come out at night to feed on snails, tadpoles, small fish, insects, and plants. Crayfish also do not like freezing temperatures. In winter, crayfish that live in water burrow into the mud. The colder the weather, the deeper they burrow.

In many parts of the world, people eat crayfish. Some fish and other animals also eat crayfish, and fishermen often use crayfish for bait.

creation

Creation is the act of making something new. Most people believe that at one time the universe did not exist. How was it made? There have been many different ideas about the creation of the universe and of life.

Jews, Christians, and Muslims believe that one God created the entire universe. He separated the light from the darkness. He created the sun, moon, and stars. He created the first plants and animals. And, finally, He made the first man and woman. You may read about this in the Bible, in the first chapters of the book of Genesis. Some people think creation happened exactly as described in Genesis. Others think Genesis is a poetic way of expressing the mystery of creation.

Early peoples had many ideas about how life began. Some spoke of a magical animal. Others believed in powerful gods. Some thought a god created all living things. Others said the god created only a certain group of humans. Many American Indian tribes have stories about gods who created their tribes.

Today, scientists wonder about how the universe began and how life started. What force or power could have created something as vast as the universe and brought the first creatures to life? Scientists have ideas about the beginnings of the universe and of living things. But the beginning of all things is still a great mystery.

See also **evolution.**

credit card

A credit card is a small plastic card that may be used in place of money in many stores, restaurants, and other places. When you buy something with a credit card, you don't have to pay for the item at that time. Instead, you receive a bill from your credit-card company each month, listing the things you have bought.

If you don't want to pay the whole bill right away, you may pay only part of it. This means that you are borrowing the rest of the money from the credit-card company. The company charges you for the use of its money. The extra charge—called *interest*—is added to your next credit-card bill.

Some credit cards may be used to buy only certain things, such as gasoline. Other credit cards may be used to buy many different things.

Credit cards are convenient. They can be used to buy things that cost more money than people have with them. People also use credit cards to avoid having to carry cash, which might be lost or stolen. If a credit card is lost or stolen, the owner can cancel the card. But credit cards must be used with care. Otherwise, people may buy more things than they can pay for. That is one reason why you must be an adult before you can have a credit card.

Creek Indians, *see* Indians, American; Indian Wars

Crete, *see* Greece, ancient

crime

A crime is a harmful action that is against the law. A person who commits a crime may be punished by being sent to jail or may even be executed—put to death.

The most common crime in the United States is stealing. One kind of stealing is called *robbery*. It occurs when someone takes something from another person by force—grabbing a purse, for instance. Another kind of stealing is *burglary*. Burglary is breaking into a property that belongs to someone else, such as a house or office, in order to steal. A third kind of stealing is *hijacking*—stealing a vehicle, such as an airplane or truck, while it is going somewhere.

Very serious crimes include kidnapping, arson, murder, and treason. *Kidnapping* means taking people against their will. The kidnappers often demand a ransom—a large sum of money—before they will return the person. *Arson* means destroying property by setting it on fire. *Murder* is causing someone else's death on purpose. People commit *treason* when they betray their country. In the United States, someone who sells U.S. military secrets to another country is guilty of treason.

Crockett, Davy

Davy Crockett was a celebrated American frontiersman. In fact, one song calls him "the king of the wild frontier."

David Crockett was born in the mountains of eastern Tennessee in 1786. When he was still a young man, Crockett fought the Creek Indians during the War of 1812, under General Andrew Jackson.

In 1817, he moved his growing family to western Tennessee. There he became known as a fearless and skillful bear hunter and a great storyteller. He was elected to the state legislature, and later, in 1826, to the U.S. Congress.

Davy Crockett once claimed that he had killed more than 100 bears in seven months.

Crockett was popular in Washington. People were amused by his buckskin clothing, coonskin cap, and backwoods speech and ways. His old commander, Andrew Jackson, was president. But Jackson and Crockett were soon arguing over a land law and how to treat Indians. Later, the people of Tennessee refused to reelect Crockett.

Angry and hurt, Crockett set out for Texas in 1835. When he got there, Texans were fighting for independence from Mexico. In 1836, the 50-year-old Crockett helped the Texans defend the Alamo. After a ten-day battle, the fort fell. The last of its 180 defenders, including Davy Crockett, were killed.

See also **Jackson, Andrew** and **War of 1812.**

crocodile, *see* alligators and crocodiles

Crusades

In the Middle Ages, thousands of European Christians went to fight in the Holy Land—the region where Jesus had lived. Their journeys and battles are known as the Crusades.

In the year 1095, the leader of the Christian church in Europe, Pope Urban II, preached to a large crowd of nobles and knights. He told them it was their duty to rescue the Holy Land from the Turks. The Turks were Muslims, not Christians. They would not allow Christians even to visit the places where Jesus had lived and died.

The nobles and knights were inspired by the Pope's speech. "God wills it!" they shouted, and they prepared for war. Before starting out, they sewed crosses on their clothing. The word *crusade* comes from the Latin word for "cross."

The Crusaders fought the Muslims to free the Holy Land, near Jerusalem.

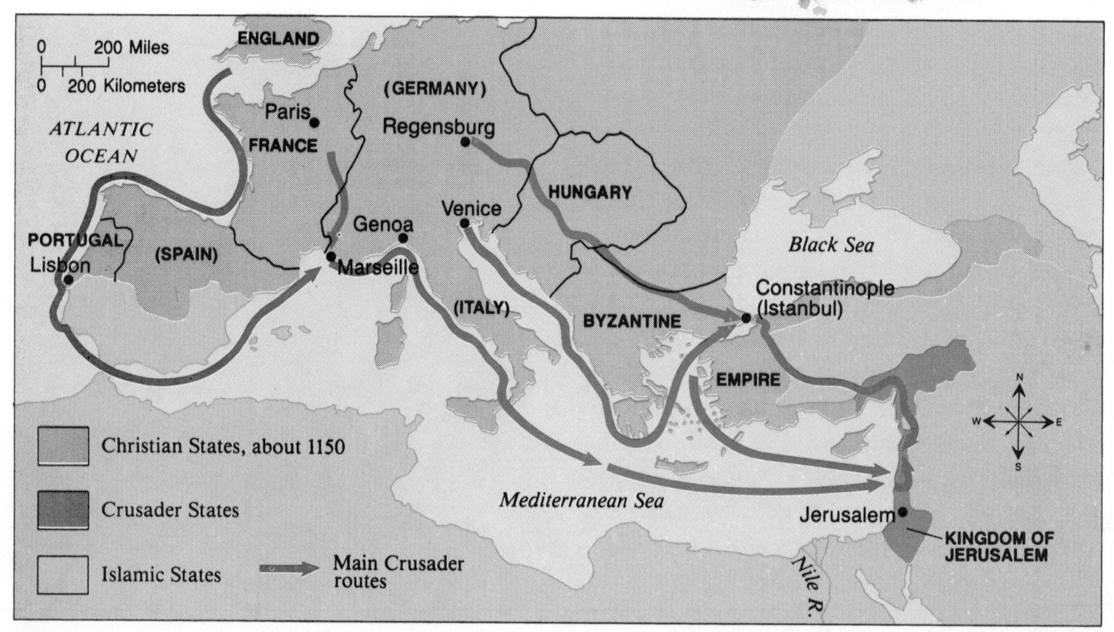

These first Crusaders fought the Turks in places that are now parts of Turkey, Lebanon, and Israel. Poorly armed bands of common people were quickly wiped out by the Turks. The armies of knights did much better. They won battles and set up small Christian kingdoms in the Holy Land.

Later, many Crusaders went home to Europe, and the Turks won back the land. The nobles formed a new army of Crusaders and went to fight again. This happened several times. In fact, there were at least eight Crusades in the 1100s and 1200s.

One of the saddest was the Children's Crusade. In 1212, thousands of French and German children left their homes to follow young leaders to the Holy Land. Many were under 12 years old. They thought they could free the Holy Land without fighting. But they never reached their goal. Some became discouraged and returned home. Cruel ship captains sold some into slavery. Most of the rest died from hunger and disease.

By 1300, the Muslims still controlled the Holy Land. The nobles decided not to form another Crusade. But the Crusades had caused changes in Europe. The Crusaders had brought back many things that Europeans had never seen, such as peaches, rice, and gunpowder. Long after the last Crusade, Europeans still traveled to the Holy Land to trade with the Muslims for these new products. Their new interest in travel led to the great age of exploration that followed.

crustacean

A crustacean (kruh-STAY-shuhn) is one of a group of animals that have no bones. Instead, they have hard shells, jointed legs, and feelers. You may have seen crustaceans in restaurants. Shrimp, crabs, and lobsters are crustaceans that are good to eat.

The name crustacean comes from *crusta,* the Latin word for shell. The crustacean's shell is made mainly of protein and a substance called *chitin.* The shell is thin and soft at the joints, so the animal can move.

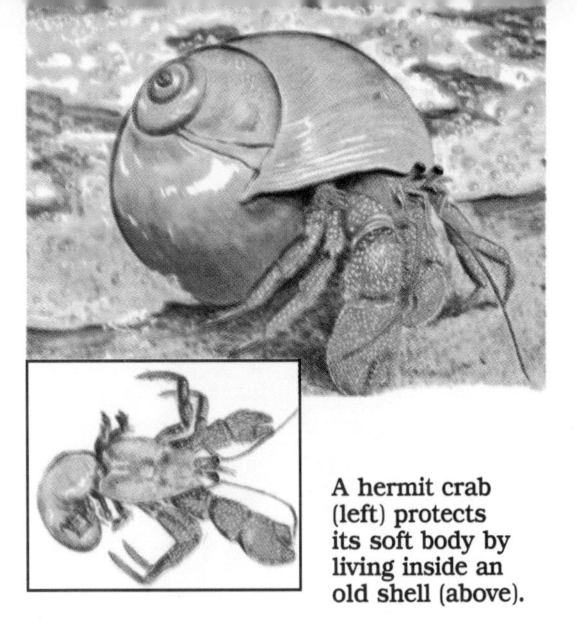

A hermit crab (left) protects its soft body by living inside an old shell (above).

The shell protects the crustacean but cannot grow. If a crustacean is growing, it must *molt*—shed its shell. A new shell forms under the old one. While the new shell is still soft and wrinkled, the crustacean has room to grow.

Many movable parts are attached to the main part of a crustacean's body. Two pairs of feelers on its head touch things around the animal and tell it about its environment. Other movable parts around the mouth hold and bite food.

Farther down the body are legs, usually 6 to 14 pairs. Some are mainly for walking or swimming. Others are *pincers* for catching food or fighting. Some crustaceans use their back legs to carry their eggs and young. If a leg breaks off during molting or in a fight, a new one soon grows in its place.

There are more than 35,000 kinds of crustaceans. The smallest are less than a millimeter long. The largest is the giant Japanese crab, which may measure 4 meters (13 feet) from the tip of one outstretched leg to the tip of the other.

Most crustaceans live in the sea. They are so common in oceans that they have been called "the insects of the sea." Some drift with the currents. They are an important source of food for fish and whales. Others live on the bottom of the oceans. Still others live at the ocean's edge. Barnacles attach themselves to the undersides of ships, piers, and rocks—or even to sharks and whales.

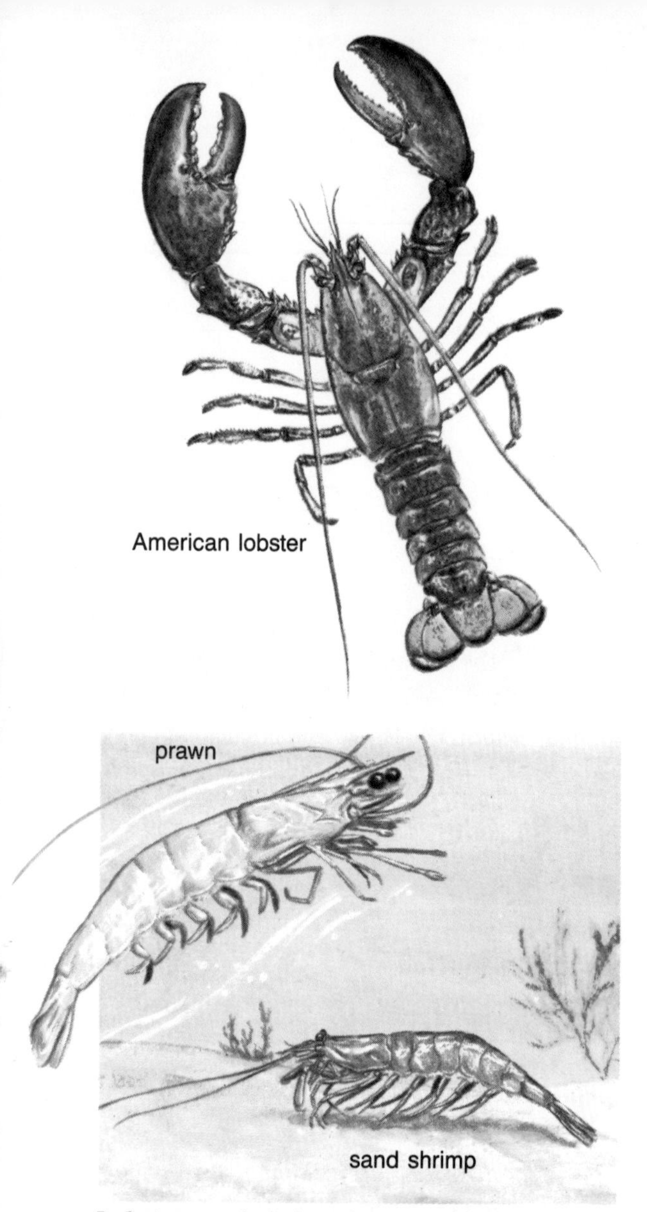

Lobsters and shrimps are two kinds of crustaceans that people like to eat.

The barnacles may live their whole lives attached to one place.

Other crustaceans live in fresh water. Water fleas—*Daphnia*—are so tiny we can barely see them without a magnifying glass. But freshwater fish can find water fleas —and eat them!

A few crustaceans live on land. The ghost crab lives in sand dunes. It hides in its burrow during the day, and comes out to eat at night. The sow bug lives under rocks and rotting logs. If it is disturbed, it curls up into a tight ball.

See also **barnacle; crab; crayfish; lobster;** and **shrimp.**

crystal

Have you ever found a piece of rock that breaks along a straight line? Have you looked at a snowflake or a grain of salt through a magnifying glass, or eaten rock candy, or admired a gem? Then you know something about crystals.

Crystals are solid, regular shapes formed by atoms or molecules. Many solids are made from crystals, but the crystals are usually too small to see without a powerful microscope. For example, metals are made from tiny crystals. Some solids, such as glass, are not made of crystals.

If a crystal forms slowly, it can be large enough to see easily. Some minerals found in the earth form large crystals. Their smooth, straight edges may be over a centimeter (½ inch) long. These crystals can be cubes or many other regular shapes. But each kind of mineral usually forms only one shape of crystal.

Snowflakes are really crystals of ice. They come in many beautiful patterns. A crystal of table salt, on the other hand, is always shaped like a cube. If some sugars are heated and then cooled gradually, they form the crystals that make rock candy.

See also **gem** and **quartz.**

Crystals of salt (top) are shaped like cubes. An amethyst crystal (bottom) is part of a rock.

Cuba

Capital: Havana
Area: 44,218 square miles (114,525 square kilometers)
Population (1985): about 10,105,000
Official language: Spanish

Cuba is an island country in the Antilles, a part of the West Indies island group. Just 90 miles (140 kilometers) south of Florida, Cuba is the largest island in the West Indies. It is about as big as the state of Pennsylvania, with almost as many people. It is so beautiful that it is called the "Pearl of the Antilles."

About a quarter of Cuba is taken up by mountains. The rest is green hills and valleys. The fertile soil and almost tropical climate are ideal for farming. But fierce summer hurricanes often damage crops and homes.

Sugar and tobacco are the major crops. Cuba also grows rice, vegetables, bananas, citrus fruits, pineapples, and coffee. Cuban factories make farm machinery, fertilizers, tools, and cement. The fishing industry is growing. Cuba ships goods to other countries from its many harbor cities including Havana, Nuevitas, Cienfuegos, Guantánamo, and Santiago de Cuba.

Christopher Columbus claimed Cuba for Spain on his first voyage to the New World, in 1492. When the United States defeated Spain in the Spanish-American War, in 1898, Cuba became independent. (*See* **Spanish-American War.**)

Still, dictators controlled Cuba's government, and big U.S. companies owned the factories. In 1959, the dictator Fulgencio Batista was defeated by a small group of rebels. Their leader, Fidel Castro, declared Cuba a communist country. The government took control of the farms and factories.

Since then, more than a million Cubans have become *exiles*—people who cannot remain in their own country. In 1961, the United States helped a group of Cuban exiles

Most Cubans live in cities, many in big housing complexes.

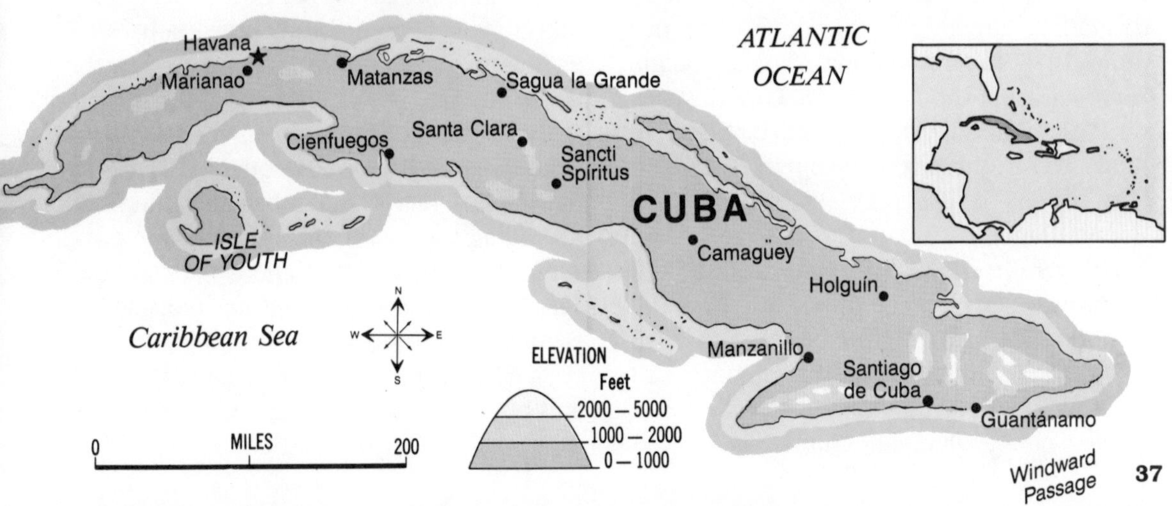

invade their homeland, but the invasion failed. The United States broke ties with Cuba in 1961 but still has a naval base at Guantánamo Bay, in southeast Cuba.

Most Cubans are white, of Spanish ancestry. Black Cubans are descended from African slaves who were brought to Cuba by the Spanish. The rest of the population is *mulatto*—a mixture of black and white.

Most Cubans live in cities. Havana, the capital, has about 2 million people. Housing is scarce, so living conditions are crowded. There are shortages of some foods. With the help of the Soviet Union, Castro is trying to improve conditions in Cuba. Education is free, and all children must attend school for at least six years.

See also **Castro, Fidel** and **West Indies.**

Marie Curie won two Nobel Prizes for her work, one in physics and one in chemistry.

Cumberland Gap

The Cumberland Gap is a natural break in the Appalachian Mountains. It enables people to cross the mountains without climbing over them. This mountain pass lies near a point where the states of Tennessee, Virginia, and Kentucky all come together.

By the mid-1700s, the land along the Atlantic coast had been settled as far inland as the Appalachians. The mountains seemed to stand as a barrier to further westward settlement. How were pioneers to get their covered wagons up and over the Appalachians?

In 1750, frontiersmen found a way. The Indians had long used a trail that passed through a gap in the Cumberland Mountains. In 1775, frontiersman Daniel Boone began clearing the Wilderness Trail through the Cumberland Gap to take pioneers to Kentucky. In the next century, 200,000 settlers crossed the Gap on their way west. (*See* **Boone, Daniel.**)

Today, railroads run through the Gap. It is surrounded by Cumberland Gap National Historical Park. This is the largest historical park in the United States, spreading over 23 square miles (60 square kilometers).

See also **Appalachian Mountains.**

Curie, Marie and Pierre

In the early 1900s, Marie and Pierre Curie were scientists in a brand-new field of physics—radioactivity. They discovered the radioactive elements polonium and radium. Both received the Nobel Prize for physics in 1903, and Marie also received the Nobel Prize for chemistry in 1911. She was the first woman to win this award. The Curies' work led the way to discovering much about the nature of the atom.

Pierre Curie was a professor at the School of Physics and Chemistry in Paris, France. In 1895, he married a promising young scientist from Poland, Maria Sklodowska. She had come to Paris to study physics, because in Poland girls were forbidden to go to the university.

Mysterious "uranium rays" had just been discovered by Antoine Becquerel. Maria—by then called Marie—soon became interested in finding the cause of these rays. First she carefully measured the energy of the rays. Then she found that uranium and another element, thorium, both had this kind of energy. She called them the "radio elements" and began to use the term *radioactivity* for the rays.

Marie tested an ore containing uranium and thorium. She found that this ore—called *pitchblende*—had more radioactivity than she expected. She did the test over and over again, with the same result. Finally, she decided there must be a new radioactive element in pitchblende.

Pierre joined Marie in the hard work of purifying the new element. After months, the Curies found enough of the new element for other scientists to examine. Marie named the element polonium, after her native Poland.

Polonium still did not account for all the radioactivity of pitchblende. The Curies realized that an even more radioactive element must exist. To find out, they had to "cook off" the impurities in tons and tons of pitchblende. After four years of hard labor, the Curies made their great discovery—the new element radium.

While the Curies purified these radioactive elements, they were being exposed to a great deal of radiation. Years later, scientists learned that radiation from radioactive atoms causes damage to human cells. The Curies were slowly being poisoned. Pierre Curie was killed in an accident in 1906. However, the exposure to radiation caused Marie to develop leukemia, cancer of the blood cells. She died in 1934.

See also **radiation; radioactivity;** and **element.**

Custer, George Armstrong

George Armstrong Custer commanded U.S. Army troops at the Battle of the Little Bighorn in Montana, in 1876. This battle is also known as "Custer's Last Stand."

Custer was born in 1839, in New Rumley, Ohio. He graduated from the U.S. Military Academy at West Point in 1861, the year the Civil War began. In the first battle of Bull Run, the young lieutenant fought bravely against Confederate cavalry. By age 23, he was a general, the youngest in the Union Army.

After the war, the U.S. Army was ordered to end Indian resistance to white settlement of the West. Custer joined in the fierce fighting. In 1876, the army learned that a large force of Sioux and Cheyenne Indians was gathering. Among their leaders were two great chiefs, Sitting Bull and Crazy Horse. Custer was ordered to take 650 soldiers and find the Indian force.

On Sunday, June 25, he found the Indian camp on the Little Bighorn River. Recklessly, he decided to attack at once. He led 225 of his men into the attack. The rest were to attack from other sides. Custer did not know that at least 2,000 Indian warriors lay hidden in the camp. They quickly wiped out Custer and every one of his 225 men.

See also **Indian Wars** and **Sitting Bull.**

Custer meets with a group of Indian leaders. He and all his men were killed near the Little Bighorn River, in 1876. They were attacking an Indian encampment.

THE THOMAS GILCREASE INSTITUTE OF AMERICAN HISTORY AND ART, TULSA, OKLAHOMA.

cycling, *see* bicycle

cycling, see bicycle

Cyprus, *see* Middle East

Czechoslovakia

Capital: Prague
Area: 49,370 square miles (127,868 square kilometers)
Population (1985): about 15,502,000
Official languages: Czech and Slovak

Czechoslovakia is a country in central Europe. It was formed in 1918 from three parts of the Austro-Hungarian Empire. Bohemia and Moravia are the homelands of the Czech people. Slovakia is the homeland of the Slovaks. Their names were combined into a single name for their new country.

Czechoslovakia is about as big as New York State and has almost as many people. Mountains, fertile valleys, and plains cover much of the country. About half the land is used to grow crops. Factories make steel, machinery, cars, and textiles. Czechoslovakia is a communist country, so the government owns the farms and factories.

Prague, the capital and largest city, is near the center of Bohemia. It is 1,000 years old and still has many beautiful old castles and palaces. Brno, in Moravia, is a steel and textile center. Bratislava, a city on the Danube River in Slovakia, is the country's most important port.

Prague, the capital of Czechoslovakia, is an ancient city. Near its center is a castle.

The earliest form of the letter *D* was the ancient Egyptian picture writing for the word *door*.

The Hebrews called this letter *daleth*, meaning "door." They drew it in the shape of a triangle.

The Greeks borrowed the letter. They changed its shape slightly and called it *delta*.

Da Gama, Vasco

The Portuguese explorer Vasco da Gama was the first to sail all the way from Europe to India. Before then, Europeans had to travel to the Indies, as they called India and eastern Asia, partly by land and partly by sea. This trip was long and very expensive.

The Portuguese thought it would be quicker and cheaper to sail to India around the bottom of Africa and across the Indian Ocean. In 1488, the Portuguese explorer Bartolomeu Dias reached the Cape of Good Hope, at the tip of Africa, before turning back.

In July 1497, Vasco da Gama set out from Portugal with four ships. He reached the Cape of Good Hope more than four months later. He sailed north along the eastern coast of Africa and stopped at East African trading ports. At Malindi, Kenya, he hired a local seaman to guide his ships across the Indian Ocean. In May 1498, Da Gama's small fleet reached the port of Calicut, India.

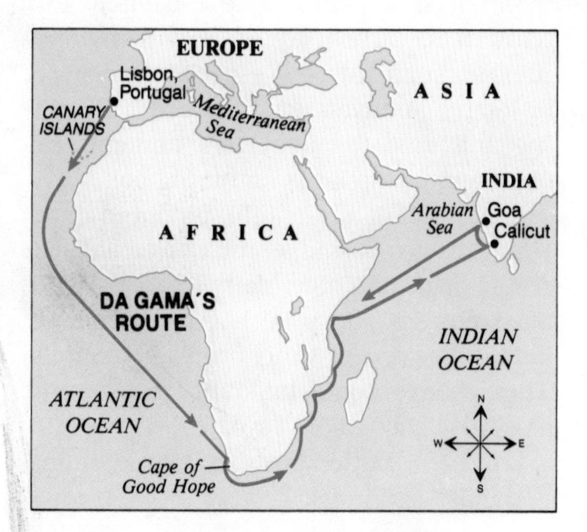

Da Gama returned to Portugal in September 1499 with a cargo of spices. The homeward voyage was very difficult. Disease killed many of the crew. But Portuguese traders finally had an all-water route to India.

Da Gama made two later voyages to India. He died there in 1524.

dairying

Dairying is the industry of producing, processing, and selling milk and its products. Your favorite ice cream, the cheese on your cheeseburger, and the butter on your pancakes are all dairy products—foods made from milk.

Dairying is big business throughout North America and much of Europe. If you put all the milk produced in the United States in one year into quart cartons and lined them up, they would circle the earth over a hundred times.

People in some parts of the world get milk from reindeer, llamas, goats, or sheep. But the most common dairy animal around the world is the cow. The major dairy cow breeds in the United States are Holstein, Jersey, Guernsey, Ayrshire, and Brown Swiss. Wisconsin is the champion milk producer of the United States, and is called the "Dairy State."

Like all mammals, a cow produces milk for her young. When a cow is regularly milked, she begins to produce more than her young need. A dairy cow produces about 12,000 pounds (5,400 kilograms) of milk a year.

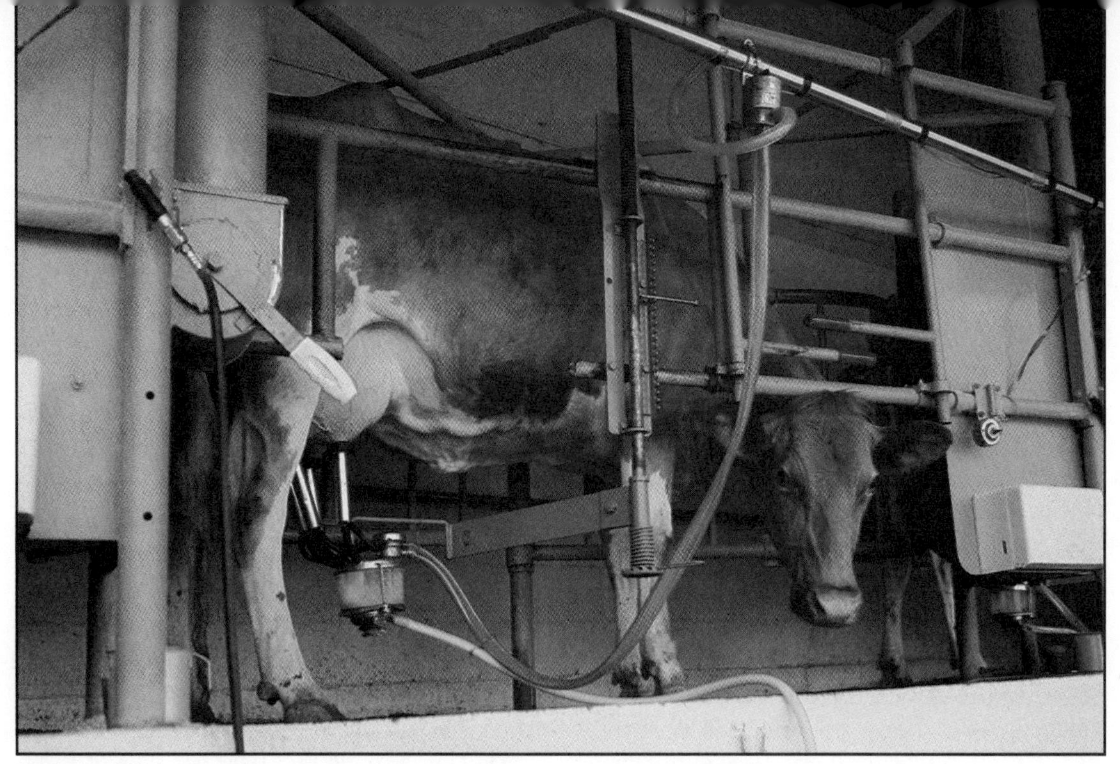

Before milking machines were invented, farmers milked all their cows by hand. Now, a single milking machine can milk four to six cows at once.

The milk is produced in mammary glands called *udders* and is made by the cow from the food she eats. Cows eat clover, alfalfa, and bluestem grasses when they graze in the pasture. When they are fed in the barn, they eat corn and hay. The kinds of foods cows eat affect the taste of their milk.

On a dairy farm, cows live in huge barns and go out to feed in a grassy pasture during good weather. The cows are milked several times each day by huge milking machines that draw the milk from their udders. A dairy farmer may milk four to six cows at a time with one machine.

The milk is then sent through a stainless-steel or glass pipe to a large tank, where it is cooled to keep it from spoiling. Sometimes, the milk is processed at the same location. Usually, it is *pasteurized*—heated to a certain temperature to kill off harmful germs. Most milk in North America is also *homogenized*. In this process, the creamy part of the milk, the *curd,* is evenly mixed with the watery portion, the *whey.* If milk is not homogenized, the cream rises and forms a layer on top of the milk. Removing the layer of cream results in a low-fat milk called *skim milk.*

After the milk is processed, it is poured into the containers in which you buy it. It may be poured into large gallon containers or the small, familiar half-pint cartons sold at school. Some milk is poured into plastic "pillows"—giant-sized bags that hold 53 pounds of milk. They are generally sold to restaurants.

All through the processing of milk, special care is taken to be sure the milk does not become contaminated with bacteria or dirt. Local health departments inspect dairies to be sure everything is clean and safe.

Milk is an important food. It contains proteins, fats, carbohydrates, and many vitamins and minerals. It is especially important to infants and children. They are still growing and need the important minerals calcium and phosphorus for strong bones.

About half of all the milk produced in the United States is sold as milk or cream. The rest is made into other dairy foods. To make most cheeses and yogurt, certain kinds of helpful bacteria or fungi are added to milk. They change liquid milk into a semisolid. They also change the flavor.

See also **cattle; farm animal; farming;** and **milk.**

Dallas

Dallas is the second-largest city in the state of Texas. Only Houston has more people than Dallas. About 30 miles (48 kilometers) east of Dallas lies the city of Fort Worth. The Dallas-Fort Worth Regional Airport is one of the busiest airports in the world.

In 1841, John Neely Bryan built a trading post on the banks of the Trinity River in north-central Texas. A village was built there in 1846. This village was probably named Dallas for George Dallas, who was then vice president of the United States, under President James K. Polk.

Today, Dallas is a business and industrial center. It is the South's most important city for banking and insurance. More oil companies have their headquarters in Dallas than in any other U.S. city. Companies that make airplanes, missiles, and computers are also located in Dallas.

Thanksgiving Square in Dallas, a green space surrounded by skyscrapers.

Millions of people have shopped at the famous Neiman-Marcus department store in Dallas. Another popular place to visit is State Fair Park, which includes many of Dallas's museums. The annual Cotton Bowl college football game is played at the Cotton Bowl, a giant stadium.

President John F. Kennedy was assassinated in Dallas in November 1963. The vice-president, Lyndon B. Johnson, took the oath of office in Dallas, and became the next president.

dam

A dam is a wall built across a river or stream to hold back the water. The water blocked by a dam spreads out to form a *reservoir*—a lake for storing water. As water collects behind the dam, the level of the reservoir rises. During dry seasons, the water level drops. Dams are specially built to allow some water to flow over or through them. The flow is controlled to help keep the reservoir at the desired level. In this way, water can be stored for many uses.

History of Dams Long before people built dams, beavers were hard at work constructing them. They use their sharp teeth to cut down trees and gnaw them into sections. They drag the sections into a slow-moving stream and pack them with mud and stones. Then they build a home in the pond that forms behind their dam. (*See* **beaver** and **animal homes.**)

Throughout history, people have had to deal with either too much or too little water. Every year, melting snows and heavy spring rains cause streams and rivers to overflow. Crops and homes are flooded, and people and animals suffer.

In other seasons and places, there may not be enough rain. Rivers and wells run dry. Crops wilt and die. People and livestock grow thirsty. Fires may rage through acres of dry forests.

To solve these problems, people have learned to copy beavers. We build dams across streams and rivers. The first ones were built thousands of years ago. They reduced the danger of floods. The reservoirs behind dams stored water for use during the dry season. A steady supply of water made it easier for people to raise crops and animals.

The ancient Romans were among the first to find other uses for the water in reservoirs. They put the water to work supplying power for gristmills—machines that crush grain and make part of it flour. The gristmills were built next to the dams. Large wooden wheels were placed in the path of the water released from the dam. The stream of water struck the blades of the waterwheel and made it turn. The waterwheel was connected to millstones inside the gristmill. As the wheel spun, it turned the millstones. The turning stones ground the grain. Later, water was also used to power sawmills and to generate electricity.

Kinds of Dams and Their Uses It is not easy to build a wall across a stream. Water is heavy. If a dam is 10 meters (33 feet) high, the water at the bottom has a pressure of 10,000 kilograms on a square meter (about a ton on each square foot). So dams must be very strong, especially near their bases.

The earliest dams were made of earth or rocks or both. Severe floods sometimes washed them away. Gradually, people built stronger and more watertight dams. They also added floodgates and spillways. A spillway may be a pipe, tunnel, or sloping concrete channel near the top of a dam. It lets excess water flow out of the reservoir. Sometimes, floodgates control the spillways. They open and close to release more or less water.

Many large dams are filled with earth. First, the water in the stream is held back by a temporary dam or directed in a different path. Then a giant wall is built from soil, clay, and gravel. These are laid down one layer at a time. Heavy rollers pack these materials together to make the wall watertight. An outer layer of rocks is added. Finally, the water is let loose to form the reservoir behind the dam.

beaver dam

If plenty of rocks are available, they are used instead of earth. To make a rock dam watertight, concrete covers the side facing the reservoir.

The tallest dam in the United States is an *earth-fill dam.* It is the Oroville Dam across the Feather River in California. The Oroville Dam is 235 meters (770 feet) high. Canada's Mica Dam on the Columbia River is a little taller. It is a *rock-fill dam* 242 meters (794 feet) tall. The longest earth-fill dam in the United States is Fort Peck Dam in Montana. It is 6.5 kilometers (4 miles) long.

Many dams were built of blocks of stone held together by cement. These *masonry dams* were built mostly across narrow valleys. Sometimes, dams were built from wood. Today, concrete is widely used, sometimes with steel supports inside.

Concrete dams are commonly used to dam up wide valleys and turn them into reservoirs. These dams are longer than they are high. On the reservoir side, the concrete wall is usually straight. On the other side, the downstream side, the wall slopes. The bottom of the dam is extremely thick. The weight of so much concrete keeps the dam from sliding or being pushed by the water behind it. Because their own weight holds these dams in place, they are called *gravity dams.* The Grand Coulee Dam in Washington is a concrete gravity dam. The tallest dam of any kind in the world is a gravity dam, too. It is the 285-meter (935-foot) Grand Dixence Dam in Switzerland.

Arch dams usually block steep, narrow canyons. The point of the arch faces upstream into the reservoir. The canyon walls help support the dam. Monticello Dam in California is an example of an arch dam.

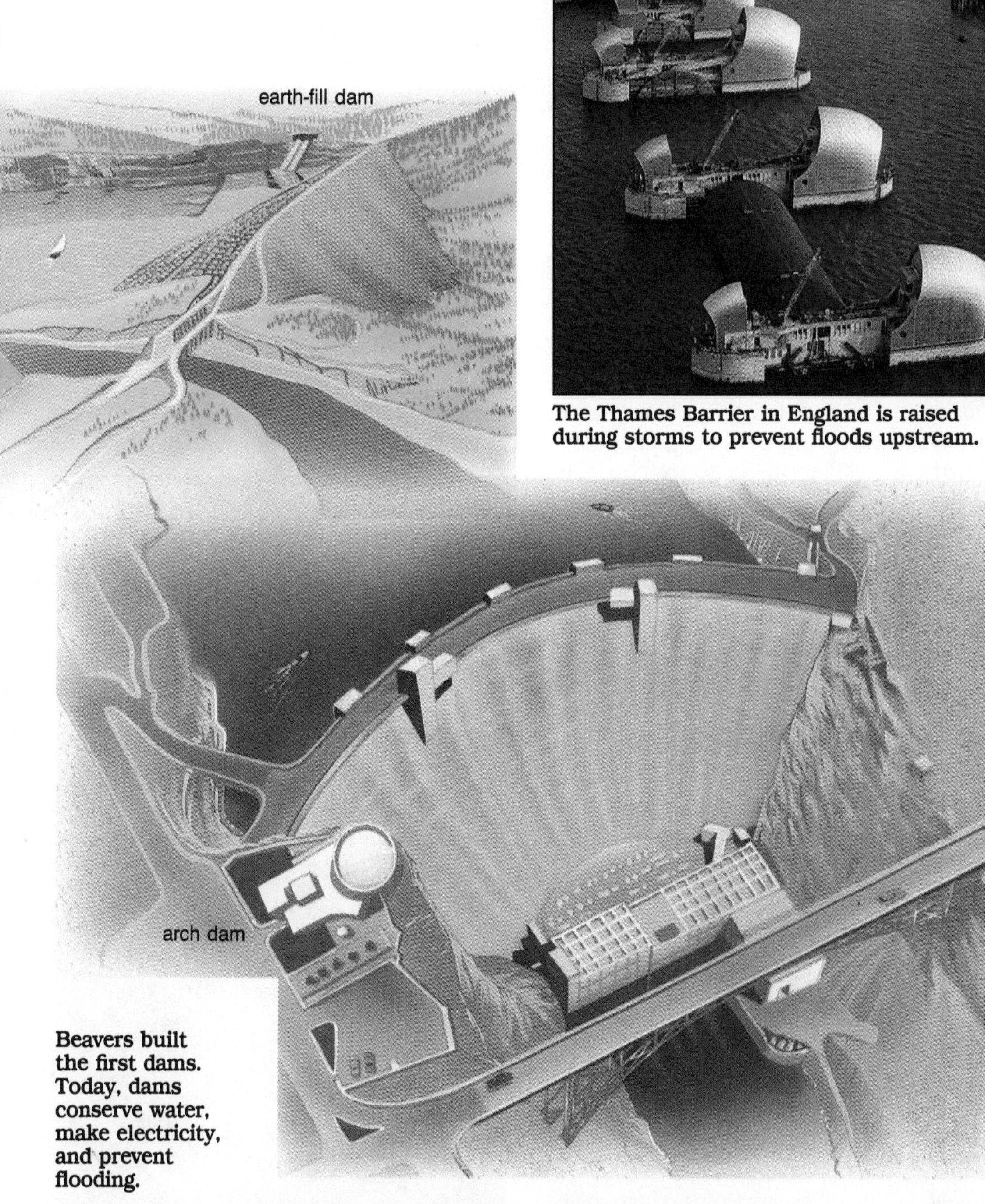

The Thames Barrier in England is raised during storms to prevent floods upstream.

Beavers built the first dams. Today, dams conserve water, make electricity, and prevent flooding.

The *movable dam* is a new kind. The first movable dam, called the Thames Barrier, was completed in England in 1982. It protects London from North Sea floodwaters that move up the Thames River. The dam has ten floodgates, each 61 meters (200 feet) across. The floodgates rest on the river bottom. When not in use, large ships can pass over them. When needed to prevent flooding, steel arms lift the floodgates into position. They form a dam more than 15 meters (50 feet) high.

Flood control saves lives and property. It also helps to conserve soil. When floods wash over farmlands, topsoil is carried away. The Nile River Valley, in Egypt, was once one of the most fertile areas in the world. Annual floods gradually washed away the topsoil. Finally, the Aswan High Dam was built to protect the farm land and provide water.

Dams also make shallow or rocky rivers usable by boats. A dam raises the level of the stream behind it. Locks like those used for canals can raise and lower ships so that they can pass over or around the dam. The 27 major dams built by the Tennessee Valley Authority in the United States make the Tennessee River deeper. Now ships can travel from the Ohio River all the way to Knoxville, Tennessee, more than 1,046 kilometers (650 miles) away. (*See* **canal.**)

Many modern dams are *hydroelectric dams.* The water stored behind them is used to produce electricity. In a hydroelectric dam, water is released so that it falls down long pipes or tunnels. At the bottom, it strikes the blades of huge waterwheels called *turbines.* The turbines are connected to generators. As the generators turn, they produce electric current. The water flows out the downstream side of the dam through another large pipe.

Hydroelectric dams are some of the highest dams. Hoover Dam, on the Colorado River, is the tallest hydroelectric dam in the United States—221 meters (726 feet). At 183 meters (602 feet), Shasta Dam in California is second. Hungry Horse Dam in Montana, and Grand Coulee in Washington are the third- and fourth-tallest.

The reservoirs behind dams are often used for swimming, fishing, and boating. Lake Mead, formed by Hoover Dam, is a national recreational area. Each year, millions of people enjoy its waters.

Disadvantages of Dams People must leave areas where reservoirs are planned. Homes, farms, and sometimes whole towns will be covered by water. Plant and animal habitats will be destroyed. The natural flow of a river is altered.

When dams fail, they cause disaster. In 1889, heavy rains caused an earth dam to collapse near Johnstown, Pennsylvania. The rushing water caused the deaths of more than 2,000 people. In 1963, a dam collapsed in Vajont, Italy. There, about 1,800 people were killed.

dance

We can see dance all around us. Performers on a television special dance in beautiful costumes. Rock stars dance while they sing. Ballet dancers tell stories through their dancing. Millions of other people dance for fun. Some enjoy square dancing or folk dancing. Teenagers go to school dances. Many others go to classes to learn tap dancing, modern dance, or ballet.

In dance, people move their bodies to express feeling and to keep time to a rhythm. Actors called *mimes* move their bodies to express feelings, but do not keep time, so they are not dancing. Soldiers march in rhythm, but they are not expressing any particular feeling, so they are not dancing, either.

History of Dance People have been dancing since the beginning of time. Early peoples believed there was magic in dancing.

Young dancers in Spain perform in the exciting flamenco style.

This pole dance in a South American village was once part of a religious ritual. In ancient times, people danced to please the gods or to ask them for things.

They danced when they needed rain or when they were about to go to war. They danced to help cure a person who was sick. They danced when they were choosing their husbands and wives. And they danced before going out to hunt.

In a hunting dance, one dancer dressed up as the animal. Others danced around him, clapping their hands or using rattles to keep time. Sometimes they chanted or sang. Their dance showed how they planned to catch and kill the animal. They believed that this would make their real hunting successful. Everyone in the village danced or watched. Children watched so they would know the dance when they grew up.

Later, many people gave up the idea that dancing was magic, but they kept dancing anyway. Some early civilizations made dancing part of their religious services. In ancient India and Greece, priests and priestesses danced during religious ceremonies. In some parts of the world, dancing is still part of religious services.

Many other people continued to dance because dancing is exciting and fun. Poor people in Europe danced on special holidays, such as May Day. Children and grown-ups put up a pole decorated with flowers and danced around it. More than 2,000 years later, people in some parts of the world still dance around a maypole each year.

Each different region of Europe developed its own dances, and many of these *folk dances* are still danced today. The Irish do *jigs* and the Scots do *hornpipes.* One exciting style of Spanish dancing is called *flamenco.* A dance popular in Poland and surrounding countries is the *polka.*

While the poor were dancing their simple dances, European kings and nobles were inventing new kinds of dance. In Italy in the 1500s, nobles began to arrange huge parties with special dances. Many of the guests dressed in beautiful costumes and performed the dances. Others sat in balconies around the sides of the room and watched.

The dances at these parties became very complicated, so the nobles looked for talented dancers who could practice dancing all the time. Some of these dancers became professional performers. They were paid to plan, practice, and perform their dances. Some of them helped invent the kind of dance called *ballet.*

At these big parties, all the guests were also invited to dance while a small orchestra played. Some dances were fast and some were slow. In some, everyone danced together. They might form two lines facing

The minuet (left) was a stately dance popular in the 1700s. The lively cakewalk (right) was developed by black Americans. It was widely popular in the 1890s.

each other. Then each dancer got a turn promenading between the lines. In other dances, the people formed "squares," two to a side. Two dancers at a time came to the middle of the square to bow or swing each other around. In other dances at these parties, men and women danced as couples. This was the beginning of *ballroom* dancing. Today's school dances are a kind of ballroom dancing, although both the dances and the music have changed.

One of the dances that became popular at fancy balls was the *minuet.* It was a stately dance in which the man and woman touched hands and bowed to each other. In the 1700s, composers wrote thousands of minuets. Music students still play famous minuets by Johann Sebastian Bach, Joseph Haydn, and many other composers. But people hardly ever dance minuets anymore.

In the 1800s, a daring new dance called the *waltz* became popular. Its music was like the minuet in some ways, but it was faster. A waltzing couple had to hold on to each other to keep from flying apart as they whirled across the floor. The home of the waltz was the city of Vienna in Austria, and some of the most famous waltzes were written by Johann Strauss, a Viennese composer. Waltzes are still popular at dances.

Dance in America The American Indians had tribal dances. Like early peoples, they believed that dancing could be magic. They danced to ask for rain, for successful hunting, and for victory in war. They used drums to keep rhythm, and sometimes the dancers chanted or sang.

The early settlers brought dancing from Europe. They brought *reels* and *square* dances. Settlers in the South also knew the minuet and other ballroom dances. Then black slaves from Africa introduced their own dances and music.

In the late 1800s, the different kinds of dances in the United States began to blend together. People still enjoyed dancing to waltzes from Europe, but they also liked the even livelier dances introduced by black Americans, such as the *cakewalk.* Soon, dance bands were playing many new kinds of music introduced by blacks, including ragtime and jazz. The new music called for still more new dances.

In the 1900s, people were inventing new dances almost every year. One was the *Charleston.* It was popular in the 1920s. From Latin America came other new dances, including the *tango* and the *mambo.* In the 1950s, dancers took up a new music called *rock 'n' roll.* There were many rock dances

Stage dancing found a home in the Broadway musical. These dancers are performing in *West Side Story,* which includes ballet and many kinds of popular dance.

with strange names, such as the *monkey* and the *boogaloo.*

Until about 1920, people who wanted to dance to music had to go to a dance hall, where there was an orchestra. After the phonograph was invented it was possible for them to dance anywhere—in school gymnasiums or even in their own living rooms. Soon, some dance halls had no live bands. They played records over loudspeakers and were called *discotheques* or *discos.*

Not everyone danced the new dances, however. Some people were interested in the old folk dances. They learned the Scots *Highland fling,* English and Irish country dances, and American square dances. People often went to square dances dressed in colorful Wild West outfits. (*See* **folk dance.**)

Dancing on Stage The United States also developed new kinds of dances for performance on stage. One of the most popular is tap dancing. Tap combines one kind of Irish dancing with new rhythms from black American music. Dancers with metal "taps" on their shoes tap out complicated rhythms to the music. (*See* **tap dance.**)

Dances for variety shows, musical comedies, and movies used different movements from modern dance and ballet. They also used tap dancing, "soft-shoe" dancing, and chorus-line dancing. Chorus-line dancing first developed in France.

Some Broadway musicals famous for their dancing were *Oklahoma, West Side Story,* and *A Chorus Line.* Movie dancers such as Fred Astaire, Ginger Rogers, and Gene Kelly became famous all over the world.

In the 1900s, the United States also became a home to ballet. This form of dancing developed in France, and later in Russia. A ballet often tells a story, and the music is played by an orchestra. Many ballets today are danced on a large stage with beautiful scenery. (*See* **ballet.**)

The greatest ballet director in the United States was George Balanchine, who emigrated to New York from Russia and France. One of the great dancers is Mikhail Baryshnikov, who came from the Soviet Union. (*See* **Balanchine, George** and **Baryshnikov, Mikhail.**)

Some American dancers in the 1920s and 1930s wanted to create a new kind of dance more free than ballet. They developed *modern dance,* exploring movement for its own sake and as creative expression. Martha Graham was an important dancer and choreographer in modern dance. Today, there are many modern dance companies. (*See* **Graham, Martha** and **Ailey, Alvin.**)

Dark Ages

Life changed for the people of Europe when the Roman Empire grew weak and crumbled after A.D. 400. This period lasted until the beginning of modern times around 1500. It is known as the Middle Ages. During the early part of the Middle Ages—from about the years 500 to 1000—life was hard. Few people were educated. This period is sometimes known as the Dark Ages.

During the Dark Ages, Europe was divided into small kingdoms. Robbers roamed the countryside. From time to time, bands of fierce invaders would swoop down on villages and destroy them. One group of invaders, the Vikings of northern Europe, were feared far and wide. (*See* **Vikings.**)

Most people lived in small farming communities called *manors.* A manor was owned by a lord and his family. The peasants who lived on a manor had to farm the lord's fields as well as their own. In return for their work, the lord protected them. Usually, he had his own small army to defend the manor from robbers and invaders. Some lords lived in castles, where peasants could stay in times of danger. (*See* **castle.**)

Peasants lived in small huts that were cold, dirty, and dark. They ate mostly black bread, vegetables, chicken, and eggs. Many peasants died of disease or were killed in battles. Very few lived past the age of 40.

The Christian Church was very important during the Dark Ages. Every manor had its priest, who conducted religious services and helped people in their daily lives. In addition, the Church set up communities like manors for men and women who wanted to devote their time to God. The men were *monks,* and their communities were called *monasteries.* The women, called *nuns,* lived in *convents.*

Monasteries and convents were places of prayer, but also provided many services. They ran the only schools of the time. They cared for the sick and took care of travelers. Monks kept libraries and copied books by hand. (*See* **monks and monasteries.**)

Gradually, the lords grew more powerful. Life became more peaceful. People were then able to spend more time thinking and creating. The Dark Ages came to an end.

See also **Middle Ages.**

Darwin, Charles

Charles Darwin is famous for his theory of evolution. He said that all living things are descendants of just a few living things that existed long ago.

Charles Darwin took a job as a naturalist on this ship, the *Beagle.* He traveled on it for five years, studying plants and animals.

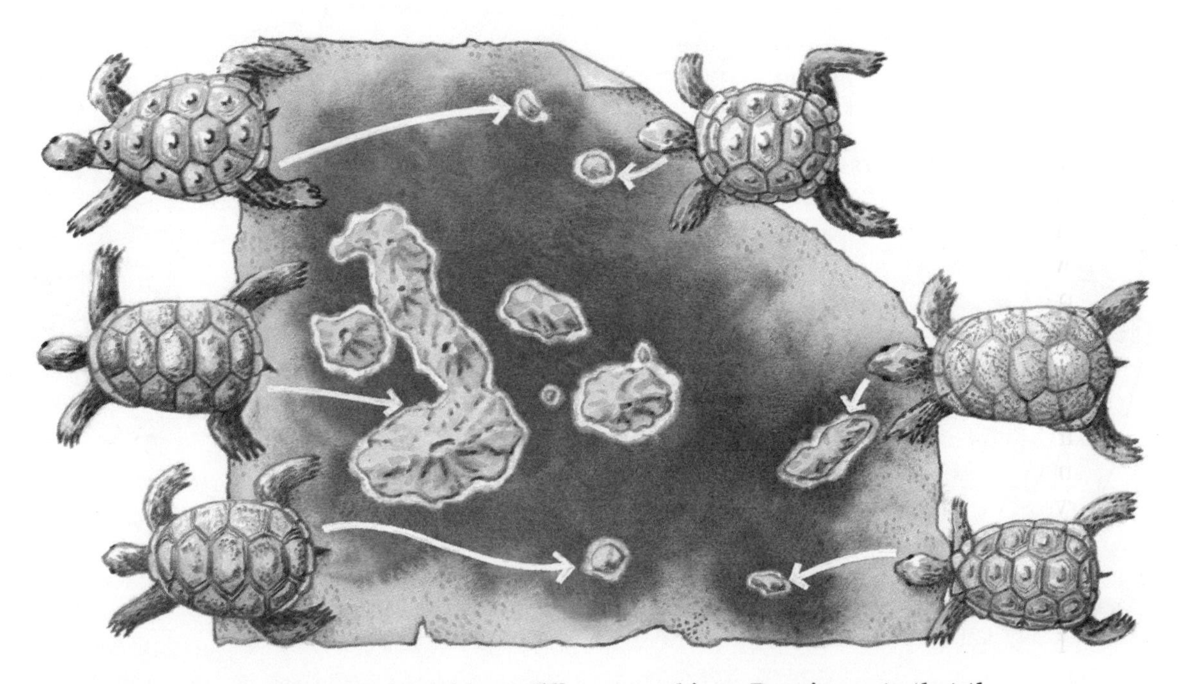

Tortoises on each Galapagos Island have different markings. Darwin wrote that the tortoises had the same ancestors, but had evolved separately for centuries.

Darwin was born in England in 1809. His grandfather, Dr. Erasmus Darwin, was well known for his writings about living things. Charles, too, studied to be a doctor, and then a minister. But his real interest was observing plants and animals. He was curious about what they did and how they lived.

In 1831, Darwin took a job on a British ship, the *Beagle.* The ship made a five-year scientific expedition to South America and parts of the Pacific Ocean. Darwin's job was to go ashore whenever the ship landed and study the living things he found there. He found hundreds of plants and animals he had never seen before. He collected many of these to take back to England.

What especially fascinated Darwin was that each living thing seemed so well suited to its environment. He found fossils of extinct animals in South America that resembled some living animal species. He realized that living things changed over time. He wondered if nature somehow chose the living things that were best suited to live in each environment.

Darwin wrote a popular book describing all that he had seen on his travels. He also continued to study the living things around him. He worked on his idea that living things change because nature selects the best of each generation.

In 1858, Darwin heard about a naturalist named Alfred Wallace. Wallace had been studying plants and animals in the East Indies and Brazil. He had noticed the same things Darwin had noticed. Together, Darwin and Wallace presented their ideas to other scientists. Darwin's book *The Origin of Species by Means of Natural Selection* was published in 1859. It convinced many scientists that the ideas of Darwin and Wallace were correct.

Darwin was also a geologist. He studied how islands were formed in the oceans. His explanation of how coral islands are formed has been proved in the last few years. (*See* **coral.**)

Darwin's ideas helped people better understand how nature works. Today, we remember Charles Darwin as a brilliant scientist. We use the word *evolution* for his ideas about how living things change. Even today, Darwin's ideas are very important to biology.

See also **evolution.**

Data processing involves putting numbers or names in different orders. A computer can help—here, it lists children in order of their ages.

data processing

Data is information. Data processing is handling information, often using machines. It can make information easier to use by organizing or summarizing it. Data processing can also be used with numbers. Adding, subtracting, multiplying, and dividing are examples of data processing.

The most modern data-processing machine is the computer. Using computers in data processing is called *electronic data processing.* Computers and other data-processing machines can be used for many things. The government uses computers to count the population and process income tax returns. Businesses use computers to make out paychecks, calculate sales, and keep track of stock. Computers can be used to make maps and charts. Engineers use computers to design ships, airplanes, bridges—even nuclear power plants. Scientists use computers to store information about experiments and perform mathematical calculations. (*See* **computer.**)

Individuals, too, use data-processing machines. Calculators and home computers are two popular kinds of data-processing machines that are used by individuals. People use them to keep track of checking accounts, make out income-tax returns, and many other tasks.

Hundreds of years ago, people put marks on sticks to keep track of numbers. Pebbles, too, were used to add, subtract, and count. In fact, the word *calculate* comes from the Latin word *calculus,* which means "pebble."

One of the first data-processing machines was the abacus. It is still used in Asia to do calculations. Most abacuses have rods or wires strung with beads. By moving the beads along the rods or wires, it is possible to add, subtract, multiply, and divide on an abacus. (*See* **abacus.**)

The calculator is another kind of data- processing machine. One of the earliest adding machines was built in 1642 by Blaise Pascal. Various improvements turned the simple adding machine into the modern calculator. Calculators can do all kinds of arithmetic, not just adding and subtracting.

Data-processing machines, especially computers, are being improved all the time. Today, there are computers that can read words and numbers. Data-processing machines are very helpful when a lot of information must be processed or when many calculations must be performed.

dates and dating

Scientists often need to know when events in the past happened or how old a rock or a fossil may be. They have found several different ways to date objects. Some ways can identify the exact year a house was built thousands of years ago. Other ways give approximate ages in millions or billions of years. We often think of a *date* as an exact day. But scientists use the term *dating* to mean finding out the approximate date or age of a thing.

Until about 200 years ago, the people of Europe and the Americas believed that the earth was only a few thousand years old. Then scientists began to study the rocks and landscapes of England, Scotland, and Wales. They soon realized that it had taken millions of years for these landscapes to form. Still, they could only guess at how many millions of years. They could figure out which layers of rock were younger or older. Usually, the younger rock was laid down on top of the older rock. But for a long time, they had no "clock" that would measure how many years old any rock was.

Uranium Dating Then, just before 1900, a Frenchman named Antoine Becquerel discovered that the atoms of certain elements, such as uranium, give off energy. This energy is called *radioactivity.* Soon, other scientists found out that as a radioactive element gives off radioactive energy, part of the element begins to change into another element. They called this process *radioactive decay.* (*See* **radioactivity.**)

Each radioactive element decays at its own rate. For instance, it takes 4½ billion years for half of the atoms in a lump of uranium to decay to lead. Then it takes another 4½ billion years for half of the remaining uranium atoms to decay. We say that the *half-life* of uranium is 4½ billion years.

Some radioactive elements have very short half-lives—only a fraction of a second. But uranium makes an ideal natural "clock" because it has such a long half-life.

A chunk of granite usually has some minerals in it that contain uranium. Scientists measure the amounts of uranium and lead in a sample—a small portion—of the granite. From this, they can figure out how long the uranium in the sample has been decaying into lead. That is how old the granite is, since the uranium minerals are part of the rock. They know that half the uranium would decay in 4½ billion years. So if one-quarter of the uranium has decayed, the rock's age is half of 4½ billion years—2¼ billion years old.

These rocky cliffs were formed in layers. The deeper the rocks, the older they are.

Potassium Dating What about rocks that do not contain uranium? For these, scientists use a different element, a radioactive variety of potassium called *potassium-40.*

Potassium-40 is present in many common minerals, such as mica and feldspar. It decays to form a gas, argon. The half-life of potassium-40 is just under 12 billion years. So, by measuring the potassium-40 and argon in a crystal of mica, scientists can calculate how old the mineral is.

Carbon Dating Uranium and potassium dating cannot be used to date the remains of plants and animals. To find out the age of bones, shells, and wood, scientists have developed a method based on the decay of a radioactive form of carbon called *carbon-14.*

Carbon-14 is found in all living things. When a plant or animal dies, the carbon-14 it contains slowly changes to normal, nonradioactive carbon. Compared with uranium or potassium, carbon-14 has a very short half-life—only 5,730 years. So, by measuring the amount of carbon-14 remaining in a piece of bone or shell, an archaeologist can calculate how old the fragment is. The carbon-14 method can be used to date samples up to 35,000 years old. (*See* **archaeology.**)

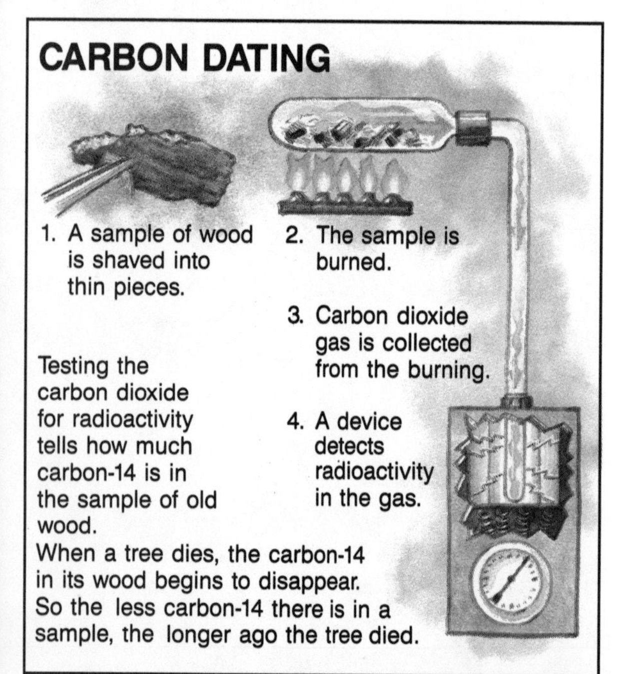

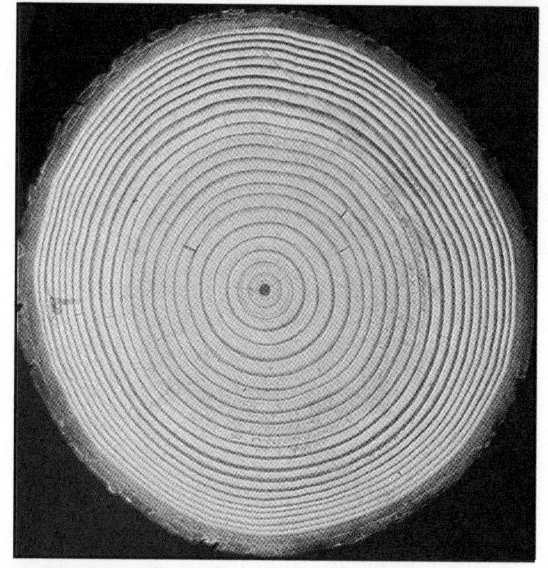

Scientists can tell how old a tree is by counting its rings—one for each year.

Tree-Ring Dating Scientists have also developed methods of dating that do not depend on radioactivity. The most familiar of these nonradioactive methods is called *tree-ring dating.*

Tree-ring dating is used to date events and changes in climate that happened up to 8,000 years ago. If you cut through a tree trunk, you will see a pattern of rings in the wood. A growing tree produces one ring every year. By counting a tree's rings, you can tell how old it is.

The width of a tree ring depends on the weather in that year—how warm or cold it was, and how much moisture the tree received. When scientists find a piece of wood from the ruins of an ancient house, they study the pattern of wide and narrow rings. Often, they can tell exactly when the tree was growing and when the ancient house was built.

See also **earth history; fossil;** and **age.**

David

David was the second king of Israel. His story is told in the Old Testament of the Bible and also in four books of the Hebrew scriptures.

The first king of Israel was Saul. David was a child when Saul led the people of Israel against the Philistines. The Philistines were a group of people who fought against Israel for control over a piece of land called Canaan.

David was born in the town of Bethlehem in the southern part of Israel. His father's name was Jesse. David worked as a shepherd, taking care of his father's flocks of sheep and goats.

David and Saul first met during Saul's war against the Philistines. Saul liked to listen to David play his lyre, a small stringed instrument that sounded like a harp. David's music made Saul feel better when he was unhappy.

David was also a great warrior. When he was still a youth, he joined in Saul's battles against the Philistines. David's most famous fight was against Goliath, the strongest of all Philistine soldiers.

Goliath was a giant who wore a bronze helmet and covered his body in armor. He challenged Saul's soldiers to fight him, but they were too afraid. So David volunteered to fight Goliath.

When the two met on the field, David was armed with only a slingshot and five stones. But David believed that God wanted him to win, and this made him strong. When Goliath charged him, David put a stone into the sling and shot it at Goliath's head. He killed Goliath with just one stone.

David became king of Israel after Saul's death. He ruled over Israel from about 1000 B.C. until about 961 B.C. David united the northern and southern halves of Israel into one kingdom. Under his rule, Israel enjoyed years of peace.

David made Jerusalem the capital of Israel. He brought the Ark of the Covenant to Jerusalem. The Ark was a small wooden box filled with precious religious objects. David's son Solomon, who became king after him, built a great and magnificent temple for the Ark in Jerusalem.

David is remembered by the Jewish people as the greatest of Israel's kings. They believe David was specially chosen by God to rule the land.

Davis, Jefferson

Jefferson Davis was the first and only president of the Confederate States of America. His presidency ran from 1861 to 1865, during the Civil War.

Davis was born in Kentucky in 1808. He grew up in Mississippi, on his family's cotton plantation. At age 16, he entered the United States Military Academy at West Point, New York.

As a lieutenant in the army, Davis fought Indians along the Wisconsin frontier. He served in the U.S. House of Representatives, but left Congress in 1846 to fight in the Mexican War. After the war, Davis became a U.S. senator and returned to Washington, D.C. In the Senate, Davis was a leading spokesman for the South and a defender of slavery. He left the Senate in 1861 when Mississippi *seceded*—withdrew—from the United States.

When the Civil War began, the southern states asked Davis to serve as president of their Confederacy. In 1865, after the South had surrendered, Davis was put in prison for two years. He died in New Orleans, Louisiana, in 1889.

See also **Civil War** and **Confederate States of America.**

Jefferson Davis served as president of the Confederate states during the Civil War.

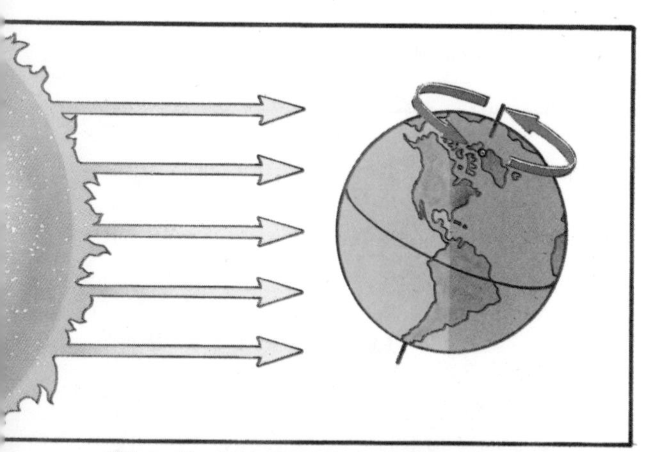

When the North Pole is farther from the sun than the South Pole, it is winter north of the equator. A far-northern town has long nights and short days.

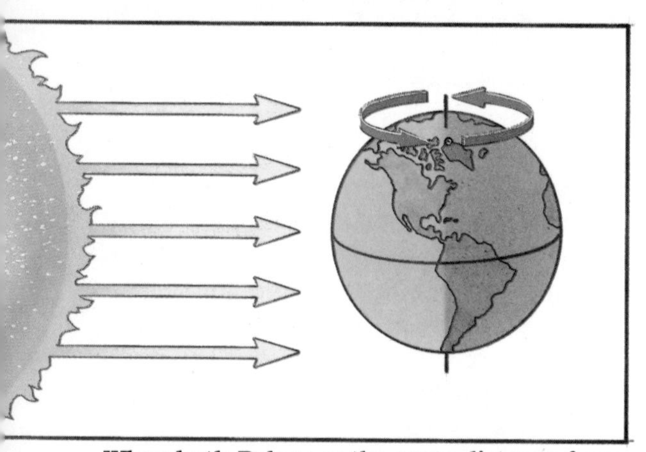

When both Poles are the same distance from the sun, all parts of the earth have days and nights of equal length. This happens about March 21 and September 21 each year.

When the North Pole is nearer the sun, it is summer in the North. The far-northern town has long days and short nights.

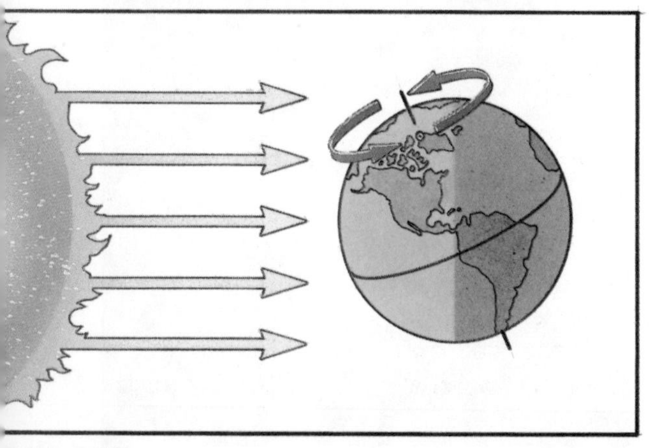

day and night

What makes day and night? You can answer this question yourself if you take a flashlight and a ball into a dark room. The flashlight is the sun. The ball is Earth. Hold the ball up so the light shines on it. Half the ball will be lighted up. The other half will be dark. Now slowly turn the ball. The half that was dark will be lighted. The half that was lighted will be dark. A tiny person standing on the surface of the ball "Earth" would see the flashlight "sun" seem to rise and set. But the flashlight is not moving. Instead, the ball is turning.

As Earth travels around the sun, it spins on an imaginary line called its *axis.* You may think of this as a line running through Earth from the North Pole to the South Pole.

If Earth were always straight up on its axis, day and night would be 12 hours each everywhere on Earth. But part of the year, the North Pole leans toward the sun. Part of the year, the South Pole leans toward it. This makes days and nights longer and shorter at different times of year in most places. In summer, days are longer than nights. In winter, nights are longer than days.

When the North Pole is leaning toward the sun, the sun shines on it all day and all night. But when the North Pole is leaning away from the sun, the sun never shines on it at all. It is dark for months.

See also **week; year; season;** and **time and timetelling.**

days of the week, *see* week

Dead Sea

The Dead Sea may be the world's saltiest body of water. It has nine times more salt than the ocean. It is also the lowest place on the earth's surface—about 1,300 feet (396 meters) below sea level. The sea is located on the border between Jordan and Israel, and is known in Israel as the Salt Sea.

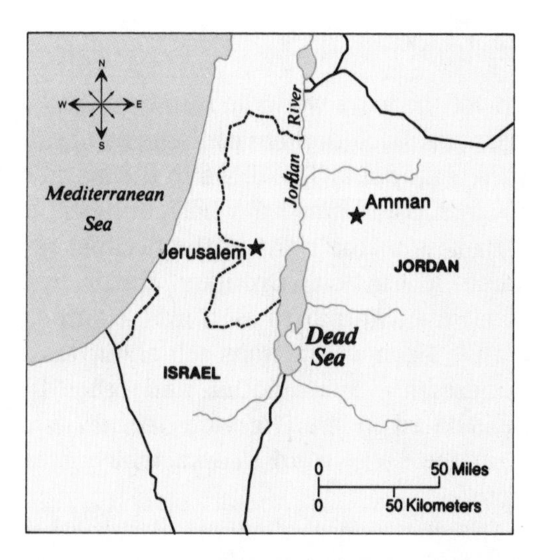

The Dead Sea is between Israel and Jordan, not far from the Mediterranean Sea. It is so salty that a swimmer can even read while floating in it.

The Dead Sea is really a lake. It is surrounded by land and has no outlet to the ocean. The Jordan River flows into its northern end.

Fish cannot live in water so salty, but many people like to swim in it. Some think the salt is healthful. Others enjoy being able to float easily. If you jumped into the Dead Sea, you would bob right up, like a cork. Some of the minerals in the Dead Sea are used to make chemical products.

Surrounding the Dead Sea are many high cliffs. About 2,000 years ago, a Jewish community lived in caves in the cliffs. In 1947, two young shepherds discovered the Dead Sea Scrolls, religious books hidden in the caves. The scrolls contain valuable information about the life of the people and religious ideas around the time of Jesus' birth.

death

Humans are probably the only animals that know they will grow old and die. Most people fear death and try not to think about it. But death, like birth, is a natural part of life. All living things eventually die.

Death can be caused by accidents or diseases. Most people die of diseases related to growing old. Death occurs when their heart and lungs stop working. The body cells are deprived of oxygen and cannot function. Sometimes, the heart and lungs start working again. This must happen quickly if it is to prevent death. Brain cells cannot recover after about three minutes without oxygen.

In the past, a person whose heart and breathing had stopped was considered dead. Today, machines can keep the heart and lungs going, so death is defined differently. A person is considered dead if no brain activity is detected for 24 hours. Any brain activity can be detected by a machine.

Doctors generally try to delay death. Some are studying death itself. Learning more about death will make it easier to meet the needs of dying people and their loved ones.

Death Valley

Death Valley is a desert region in east-central California. It is over 130 miles (210 kilometers) long. One spot in the valley is the lowest point in all of North America and South America—282 feet (86 meters) below sea level.

Indians who once lived in Death Valley called it "Ground Afire." It heats up to about

In Death Valley, only 2 inches (5 centimeters) of rain falls each year.

125° F (52° C) on hot summer days. One day in 1913, the temperature in Death Valley reached 134° F (57° C), the hottest ever recorded in the United States.

In 1849, on their way to California to look for gold, some people got lost in Death Valley. Many of them died. One who was finally rescued looked back and said, "Good-bye, death valley." This is how the valley got its name.

During the late 1800s, silver, gold, and borax were mined in the valley. Borax is used to make soap, glass, and other products. The borax was hauled from the mines to the railroad in wagons pulled by teams of 20 mules.

In 1933, Death Valley was made a National Monument. A small part of the monument is in the state of Nevada. Many people visit Death Valley during the cooler winter months.

See also **desert.**

decathlon, *see* track and field

decimal

One of the ways we write numbers is to use decimals. Each decimal contains a dot called a *decimal point.* The digits to the left of the decimal point name a whole number, and the digits to the right of the decimal point name a fraction. Ordinary fractions tell about such numbers as thirds, eighths, or tenths. Decimal fractions tell about tenths, hundredths, thousandths, and other fractions based on ten. The word *decimal* comes from the Latin word *decem,* which means "ten."

The first place after the decimal point stands for tenths. So 0.7 is seven-tenths—the same fraction as 7/10. The hundredths place comes after the tenths place, so 0.07 means seven-hundredths—7/100. And 0.17 is the same as 17/100.

When you read a number with a decimal point, you say "and" for the decimal point. For 6.7, you say "six and seven tenths."

We use decimal fractions every day to read and write dollars and cents. If the price tag on a shirt says $14.25, we know that the whole number on the left is 14 dollars. The decimal on the right means 25 cents—the same as 25-hundredths of a dollar.

Our money system uses decimals. One cent is one-*hundredth* of a dollar. This amount is 3 dollars and 40-hundredths, written $3.40.

Declaration of Independence

The Declaration of Independence is one of the most important documents in American history. In it, the 13 original colonies announce that they consider themselves free of the British government, and that they have the right to rule themselves.

The Declaration grew out of troubles that arose between the American colonists and the British government under King George III. After the French and Indian War ended in 1763, Britain tried to strengthen its control over the colonies in America. At the same time, the colonists began to demand a voice in how they were governed.

The British decided to tax the colonists and use the money to keep part of the British army in America. The colonists thought the taxes were unfair. Then the British refused to allow them to move into the Ohio Valley and other lands won in the French and Indian War. Many colonists thought the time had come to form their own nation.

In 1774, leaders chosen in the colonies met at the First Continental Congress. They agreed not to trade with Britain and to meet again in a year if things didn't improve. By 1775, Massachusetts colonists were already battling with the British. The Revolutionary War had begun. In June 1776, the men who had met at the Second Continental Congress decided to write a document explaining the colonists' beliefs about their government.

Five men were chosen to prepare the document, including Benjamin Franklin, John Adams, and Thomas Jefferson. The job of writing the declaration fell to the young Jefferson. His words soon became world famous. He wrote that people have the right to change or destroy a government that does not grant them their basic rights. He stated that every human being has the right to live, to be free, and to look for happiness.

Congress approved the Declaration of Independence on July 4, 1776. It was signed by 56 members of the Congress. The first to sign was John Hancock, the president of the Congress. He wrote his name in very large letters. "There," he said. "The king of England can read it without his glasses!"

John Adams suggested that the anniversary of the Declaration of Independence be celebrated every year "with pomp and parade, with shows, games, sports, guns, bells, bonfires, and illuminations, from one end of the continent to the other, from this time forward forevermore." And that is very much how the Fourth of July is celebrated to this day. (*See* **Fourth of July.**)

The Declaration of Independence, written by Thomas Jefferson, has inspired other nations to seek their independence, too.

> We hold these Truths to be self-evident, that all Men are created equal, that they are endowed by their Creator with certain unalienable Rights, that among these are Life, Liberty, and the Pursuit of Happiness—

deer and antelope

You may know a song that calls the American West the land "where the deer and the antelope play." There are deer and antelope in the West, but they are also found everywhere on Earth except Australia and Antarctica. Deer are a family of mammals in which the males shed their horns each year. Antelope are part of a larger family of mammals that have permanent horns. We think of deer and antelope together because they are very similar.

Deer and antelope stand on their toes. At the end of the toes on each foot is a hoof. The hoof has a hard outside and a soft inside. It protects the toes.

Deer and antelope are *herbivores*—plant-eaters. They eat grasses, leaves, and twigs. Like cattle, they have more than one stomach, and they "chew their cuds." They partly chew their food and then swallow it. It goes into one of the stomachs and is partly digested. Then the animals cough up balls of the partly digested food. These balls are called *cuds.* The animals chew the cuds some more, then swallow them again. This happens over and over.

Each summer, a deer's new antlers grow and harden.

Most deer and antelope live in groups called *herds.* A herd may have only a few animals, or it may have several thousand! Living in a herd helps protect the deer and antelope against predators—animals that hunt other animals for food. It is harder for a predator to attack an animal that is part of a group. Also, while a herd feeds, some of its members always keep watch. They warn the others if a predator approaches. When this happens, the deer or antelope run off. They can run very fast. This is their most important way of escaping predators.

The pronghorn, also known as the American antelope, lives in western North America.

There are about 40 kinds of deer. They can be placed in eight groups: true deer, American deer, musk deer, water deer, barking deer, roe deer, moose, and caribou. The smallest is the pudu, which lives in South America. It is only 37 centimeters (14½ inches) tall at the shoulders. The largest deer is the moose. It may be 229 centimeters (90 inches) tall at the shoulders.

The males of most kinds of deer grow horns made of solid bone. These are called *antlers.* In some deer, the antlers have many branches. The antlers are used when fighting other males. They also are used to fight predators. While the antlers are growing, they are covered with a thin layer of skin called *velvet.* Blood vessels in the velvet carry food and oxygen to the growing antlers. When the antlers stop growing, the velvet dries and the animal rubs it off. In late winter or spring, deer shed their antlers. Then new antlers begin to grow. Each year, deer grow new antlers.

The only female deer that grow antlers are female caribou. Caribou are also called *reindeer.* They have been tamed by the Lapps, who live in northern Scandinavia. The Lapps use reindeer to pull sleds. They eat reindeer meat and use the skin to make warm clothes.

There are about 100 kinds of antelope. Most are slim and graceful. The smallest is the royal antelope. It is about 25 centimeters (10 inches) tall at the shoulders. The largest is the giant eland. It may be 180 centimeters (6 feet) tall at the shoulders.

Almost all antelopes, including the females, have horns. The horns are hollow and do not branch. Unlike deer, antelope do not shed their horns. Different kinds of antelopes have horns of different sizes and shapes. Some are shaped like a corkscrew. Some curve backward. Some are short and straight. Some are long and very sharp. Most antelope have one pair of horns. But the male four-horned antelope has two pairs of short horns, one behind the other.

See also **moose and elk.**

Degas, Edgar

Edgar Degas (deh-GAH) was a great French artist who lived from 1834 to 1917. He did his most important work in the late 1800s.

Degas was born in Paris. When he was 20, he traveled to Italy and studied the art of the old Italian masters. He practiced drawing and became very skilled. By 1859, he felt he had completed his training.

At first, Degas hoped to do historical paintings. He soon changed his mind and became an *impressionist.* He drew everyday people and events. He used line and color to show a person or scene as if at a glance. Degas liked to show people at the racetrack, in shops, and at home. He drew and painted them just as they might be when they didn't know they were being watched.

Degas's best-known paintings and drawings are of young ballet students. He produced many oil paintings and pastel drawings of young girls in the dance studio. He also made statues of the dancers, so he could study how they looked from every point of view. He never meant for the statues to be shown. Today, however, they are exhibited in several museums, and his paintings are among the most valuable in the world.

Dancers were among Degas' favorite subjects. This pastel is *Dancer with Bouquet.*

Delaware

Capital: Dover
Area: 2,044 square miles (5,294 square kilometers) (49th-largest state)
Population (1980): 595,225 (1985): about 606,711 (47th-largest state)
Became a state: December 7, 1787 (1st state)

Delaware, on the mid-Atlantic coast, is the second-smallest state in the United States. Only Rhode Island is smaller. Delaware measures only 96 miles (154 kilometers) from north to south, and 35 miles (56 kilometers) from east to west at its widest point. It is also one of the smallest states in population. Only Vermont, Wyoming, and Alaska have fewer people than Delaware.

Delaware's nickname is the "First State." This is because it was the first state to accept the United States Constitution. Thomas Jefferson once said that like a diamond, Delaware is small but has great value. For this reason, Delaware is also known as the "Diamond State."

Land The state of Delaware is shaped like a slipper. Its rounded toe points north to Pennsylvania. Its flat sole and heel face Maryland to the west and to the south. The top of the slipper faces east, to the Delaware River, Delaware Bay, and the Atlantic Ocean. New Jersey lies across the Delaware River and Delaware Bay. Delaware, Maryland, and Virginia form the Delmarva Peninsula—a name combining parts of the names of the three states.

Large ships travel up the wide Delaware river to Philadelphia in Pennsylvania, and to ports in New Jersey. The Chesapeake and Delaware Canal cuts across the state and connects the Delaware River with Chesapeake Bay to the west.

Forests cover one-third of Delaware. There are rolling hills in the north, but most of the state is very flat. Rich soil and flat land make Delaware ideal for farming. There are farms throughout the state, but the best ones are in the south. Soybeans, corn, barley, and wheat are among the crops raised. Delaware is also a leading producer of broilers—chickens 9 to 12 weeks old.

Many of the nation's biggest companies have headquarters in Delaware. E.I. du Pont de Nemours and Company, commonly known as Du Pont, is the world's largest chemical company. One out of every three factory workers in Delaware works for Du Pont. The company was founded in 1802 by Éleuthère Irénée du Pont. Since then, the Du Pont family has played an important role in the history of Delaware.

People Most of Delaware's people live in or near cities. Wilmington is the state's largest city. Wilmington is known as the "Chemical Capital of the World" because Du Pont and several other chemical companies have their main offices there.

Newark is Delaware's second-largest city. Dover, the capital of Delaware since 1777, is in the center of the state and is surrounded by farmlands. The making of paper products is important to both Newark and Dover. Rubber, textiles, and leather are other products of Delaware's cities.

History The first inhabitants of Delaware were the Algonquian Indians. In 1609, the English explorer Henry Hudson sailed into Delaware Bay from the Atlantic Ocean. A year later, people from the British colony of Virginia sailed into Delaware Bay and up the Delaware River. They named the river and bay De La Warr, after Baron De La Warr, the governor of Virginia. Soon his name was used for the land as well.

The Dutch built the first settlement in Delaware in 1631. It was soon destroyed by the Indians of the area. Swedish settlers arrived in 1638 and built Fort Christina on the site of present-day Wilmington. Eventually, Delaware later became a British colony. To this

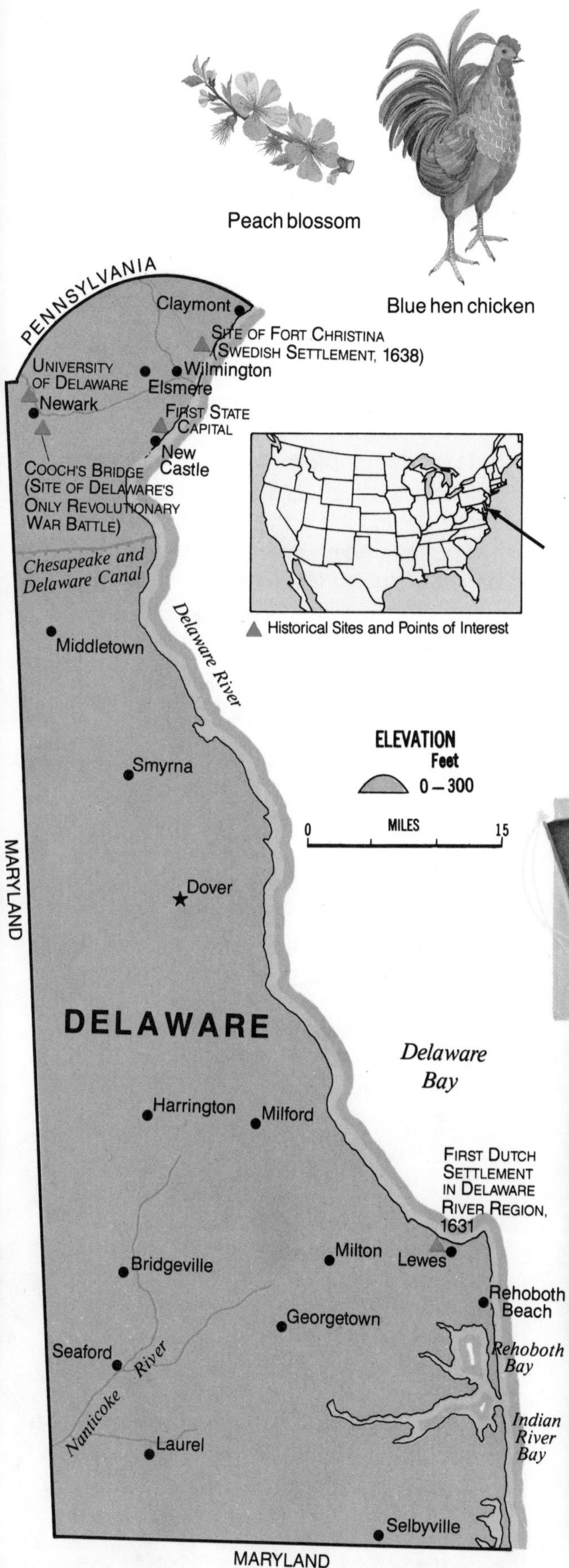

day, however, the people of Wilmington celebrate Swedish Colonial Day.

Delaware escaped most of the fighting during the Revolutionary War. By the middle of the 1800s, the Chesapeake and Delaware Canal had been completed, and railroad lines were crisscrossing the state.

Almost all of the slaves in Delaware had been freed before the Civil War began in 1861. Delaware, which lies between the North and the South, stayed in the Union. Some men from Delaware, however, fought in the Southern army.

The story of Delaware in the 1900s has much to do with the Du Pont Company. During World War I, the company made more than a billion dollars' worth of gunpowder. Du Pont used this money to set up chemical, plastics, and other businesses. Nylon, Teflon, Dacron, and artificial rubber were all developed by Du Pont. Today, Delaware is also becoming an important center for computer companies.

Rehoboth Beach is on Delaware's Atlantic shore. People come from many surrounding states to enjoy the sun and the cool ocean breezes.

A delta is a low-lying region of land crisscrossed by channels of water.

delta

A delta is a flat land region that forms where a river empties into a large body of still water. The land forms from the soil that the river leaves behind.

All rivers carry *sediment*—particles of sand, gravel, clay, and plant material taken from the land. The faster a river is flowing, the more sediment it can carry.

As the river empties into a quiet body of water, such as a lake or gulf, its water slows down suddenly. The sediment it is carrying begins to fall to the bottom. As time passes, the sediment piles up.

A very large river, such as the Nile or the Mississippi, may leave many tons of sediment at its mouth each day. A huge delta builds up. To get to the sea, the river cuts many channels through the delta. Often, the channels branch out in a fan-shaped pattern as they reach toward the sea.

The Nile Delta has been famous from the earliest days of civilization. On a map, it looks something like a triangle. It was called the *delta* because the Greek capital letter *delta* looks like a triangle. Not all deltas have this shape, but they have kept the name.

See also **erosion** and **river.**

democracy

Democracy is a form of government in which the people rule. In the words of Abraham Lincoln, it is a "government of the people, by the people, for the people."

In small communities, all the people can meet in one place to make laws. This system, called *direct democracy,* was used in the city of Athens in ancient Greece. Today, some small New England towns practice direct democracy by holding town meetings.

In large communities, there are too many people to meet all at once. People elect others to make decisions for them. This system is called *indirect democracy,* or *representative democracy.* In the United States, for example, the people elect a president and members of Congress to run the government for them.

Democracy is built on *majority rule.* This means that everyone must accept what most of the people decide in an election. The majority must consider the wishes of the minority, but everyone must obey the laws.

For a democracy to work, people must be able to speak freely, meet together openly, and communicate their ideas through newspapers, books, radio, and television. People must also express their views by voting.

First-time voters learn to make their choices on a voting machine.

Denmark, *see* Scandinavia; Europe

dentistry

Dentistry is the science of healing the teeth and other parts of the mouth. When you go to the dentist's office for a checkup, the dentist carefully examines your mouth. The dentist may take X-ray pictures of your teeth to discover any hidden problems.

The most common dental problem is a small hole in a tooth, called a *cavity.* Cavities are caused by mouth bacteria. These bacteria produce acids that dissolve parts of the tooth. The partly dissolved material, called *decay,* must be removed. The dentist cleans out the decay and smooths the hole with a drill. Then the cavity is filled to prevent further decay. Sometimes the dentist uses an anesthetic, but drilling is almost always painless.

If a tooth has been badly damaged, it may be removed. The dentist replaces it with an artificial tooth. But most dentists prefer to keep a natural tooth if possible. If the nerves are diseased, the dentist removes the nerve tissue but leaves the tooth in place. This process is called *root canal therapy.* If the nerves of the tooth are still healthy, the dentist may cover the entire tooth with a *crown.* The crown, also called a *cap,* looks just like a real tooth.

Dentists also treat diseases of the gums. Gum disease is usually caused by the buildup of a substance called *plaque.* Plaque is a sticky film that forms on the teeth when bacteria feed on food particles. If it is not cleaned off the teeth often, it begins to irritate the gums. It can also harden into a substance called *tartar* that pushes against the gums. When this happens, the teeth may become loose and fall out. You can help prevent gum disease by brushing and flossing often. You should have a dentist or dental hygienist clean the tartar off your teeth at least twice a year.

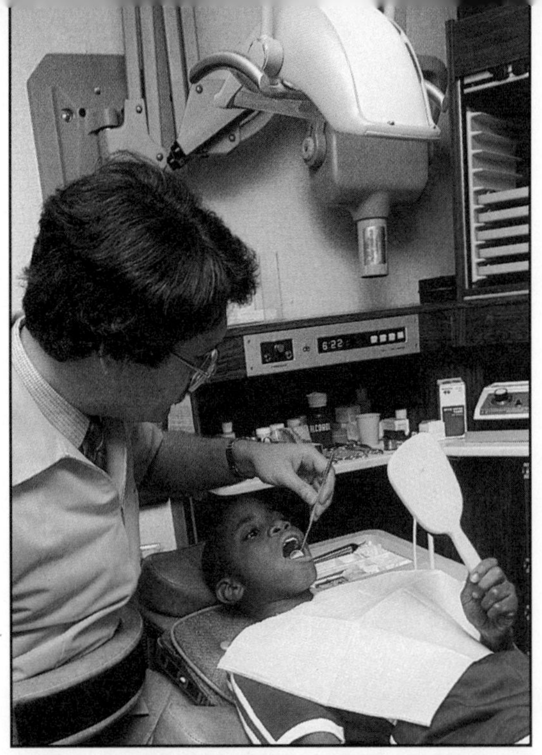

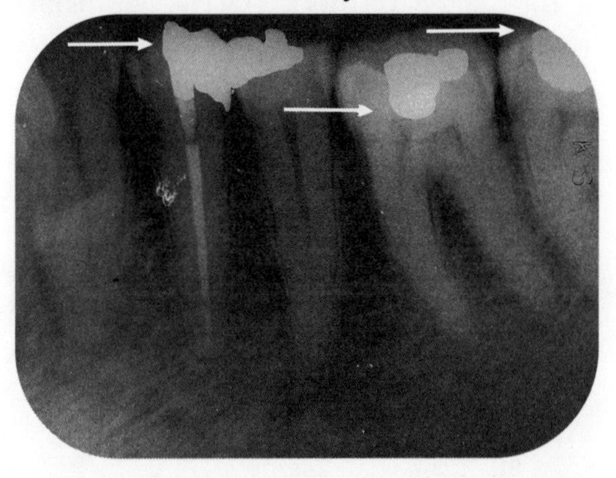

Above, a dentist examines a boy's teeth. Below, an X ray of teeth shows where cavities have been filled by a dentist.

Some dentists, called *orthodontists,* specialize in correcting the positions of teeth. Sometimes, teeth are too crowded or spaced too far apart. Chewing may be difficult, and the teeth may decay more easily. Orthodontists use braces to pull the teeth gradually into the proper position.

One of the most important services that dentists provide is preventive dentistry. Dentists show you how to brush and floss your teeth. They tell you what foods to eat or stay away from to keep your teeth healthy. With your dentist's help, you can have strong, healthy teeth and gums that will serve you well for the rest of your life.

See also **teeth.**

Denver

Denver is the capital and largest city of Colorado. More than half of Colorado's 3⅓ million people live in or near Denver. Denver is in north-central Colorado, where the Great Plains meet the Rocky Mountains.

Denver's location has made it an important transportation center. Cattle are prepared for market at the Denver Union Stockyards. Denver is home to several food and energy companies. Yet more of Denver's people work for the U.S. government and the Colorado state government than any private company. About 200 offices of the U.S. government are located in Denver. The Denver mint makes almost 7 billion coins a year.

Denver was founded by gold prospectors in the 1850s, when Colorado was still a part of the Kansas Territory. The city was named for James Denver, the governor of the territory. Denver became the capital of Colorado in 1876, when Colorado became a state.

Denver is a mile (1.6 kilometers) above sea level, and is often called the "Mile High City." But the millions of people who visit Denver each year know it as the "Gateway to the Rockies." From Denver, it is only a short trip to the parks, campgrounds, and ski resorts of the Rocky Mountains.

depression

A depression occurs when business is very slow and many people lose their jobs. In the 1930s, the United States suffered a business slowdown so severe that people called it the Great Depression. It was a time of great hardship for millions of people, not just in the United States but around the world.

The causes of the Great Depression can be traced back to the 1920s. Farmers lost money because they grew more food than they could sell. Some families even lost their farms because they could not repay money they had borrowed from banks.

American business grew quickly during the 1920s. Soon, they were making more goods than people could buy. Some factories then slowed production. Some closed down. This left many workers without jobs.

When banks closed in the Great Depression, many people lost their life savings.

Meanwhile, people who had money looked for ways to increase their savings. Some bought shares of companies. Paper certificates called *stock certificates* or *stocks* stated how many shares a person owned. When the company did well, the value of the stock increased. When business was bad, the value of the stock dropped. (*See* **stocks and bonds.**)

As more and more factories closed, the stocks of companies began to drop in price. People who owned the stocks started to panic. In October 1929, everyone began selling their stocks at once. Stock prices fell sharply, and many people lost all their money. Many banks were forced to close.

By 1932, one person in four was out of work. People lost their savings and their homes. The homeless lined up for free food given out by "soup kitchens." Families lived in shacks made of cardboard boxes.

Many lawmakers in Washington, D.C., did not realize at first how bad the depression really was. Officials hoped that business would find a way to cure itself.

In 1932, Franklin D. Roosevelt was elected president. Promising a "New Deal" for the people, Roosevelt asked Congress to pass his programs to help the country recover. One program made it possible for the banks to open again. Another put young men to work fixing up the nation's parks and forests. Other New Deal programs kept farmers from losing their farms, and families from losing their homes. There were also programs to help businesses create more jobs.

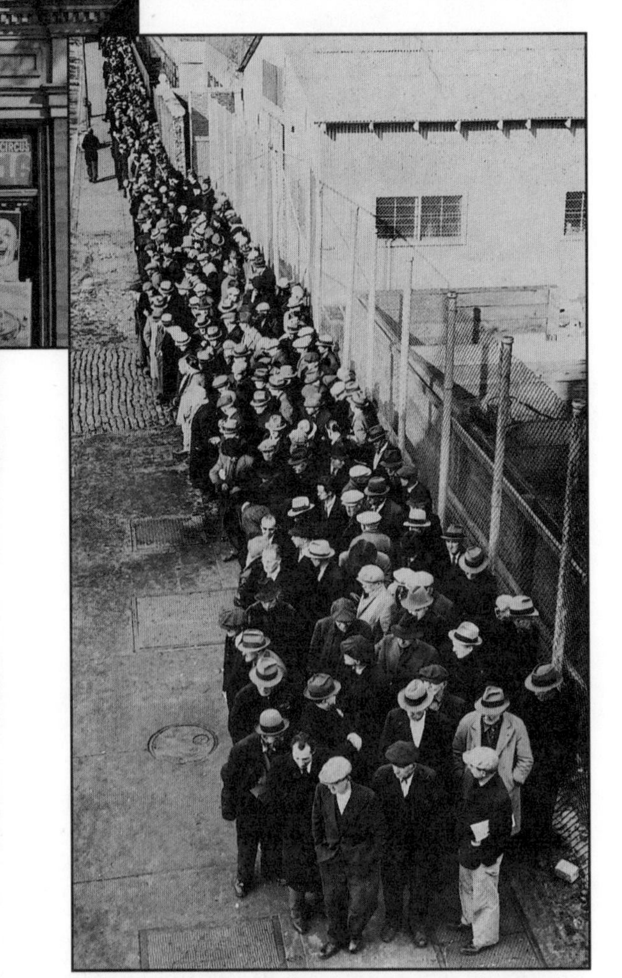

During the Depression, men without jobs waited in long breadlines to get free food.

The worst of the Great Depression was over by the late 1930s. But the memory of those hard times has lived on.

See also **Roosevelt, Franklin D.**

desert

A desert is an area of land that gets very little moisture. Land that receives less than 25 centimeters (10 inches) of rain a year is called a desert. But this does not mean that a desert receives rain each year. Some desert areas of Mexico go for several years with no rain. An area of the desert in northern Africa got no moisture for 20 years. It is believed that some parts of a desert in Peru get no rain for hundreds of years.

Deserts occupy one-fifth of Earth's surface. There are deserts in North America, South America, Asia, Africa, Australia, and Antarctica. The world's largest desert is the Sahara, which stretches across northern Africa. It covers about 9 million square kilometers (3½ million square miles)—an area about the same size as the entire United States. The smallest desert is the Atacama-Peruvian desert, in South America. It is about 360,000 square kilometers (140,000 square miles)—almost the size of the state of Montana. The desert of North America is medium in size. It includes about 1,294,000 square kilometers (500,000 square miles) of the southwestern U.S. and Mexico. The Mojave is part of this desert. The table on this page shows the desert areas of the world and their sizes.

LARGEST DESERTS OF THE WORLD

Desert	Location	Size: Square Kilometers	Size: Square Miles
Sahara	North Africa	9,000,000	3,500,000
Australian	West-Central Australia	3,400,000	1,300,000
Arabian	Southwest Asia	2,300,000	900,000
Turkistan	West-Central Asia	1,950,000	750,000
North American	Southwestern U.S.; Northwestern Mexico	1,294,000	500,000
Patagonian	Southern Argentina	670,000	260,000
Thar (Great Indian)	Northwestern India; Pakistan	595,000	230,000
Kalahari	Southwestern Africa	570,000	220,000
Takla Makan	Western China	520,000	200,000
Iranian	West-Central Asia	390,000	150,000
Atacama-Peruvian	Western South America	360,000	140,000

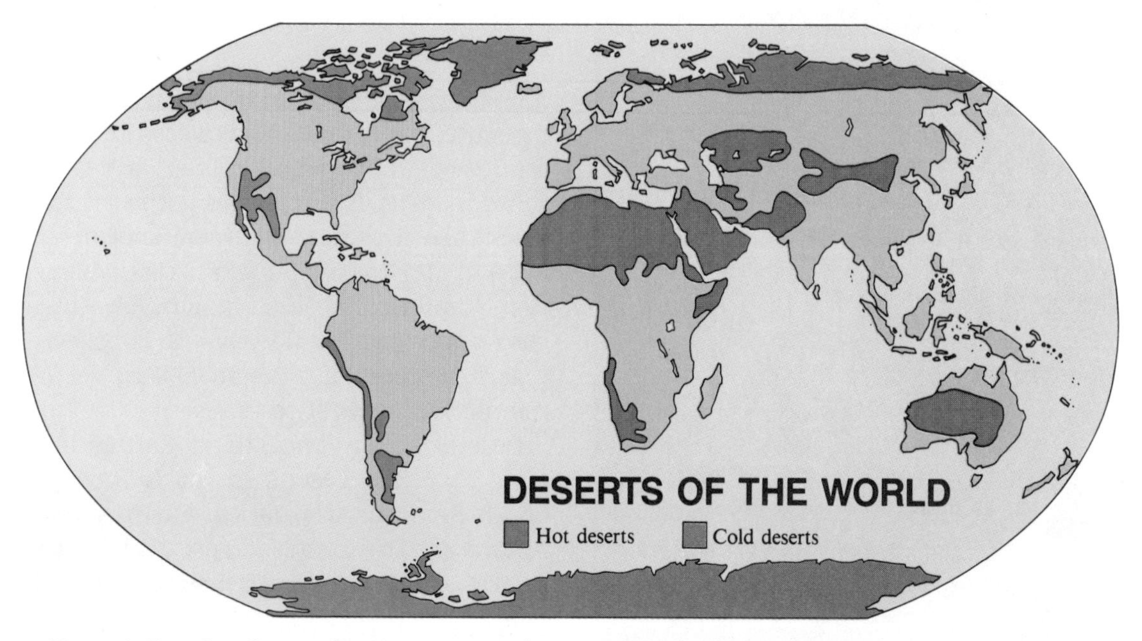

Desert Lands Some deserts are sandy, but some are not. In fact, some deserts have very rich soil. Only an eighth of the world's desert area is covered with sand. The largest area of sand in the world is part of the Arabian Desert. It is called the Empty Quarter and covers about 647,500 square kilometers (250,000 square miles)—about one-third of Saudi Arabia.

Sandy deserts have *dunes*—hills of sand. The wind forms dunes by blowing the sand into large piles. The wind also causes the dunes to move, but very slowly. White Sands National Monument in the state of New Mexico is famous for its dunes. Some of the world's largest dunes are in the Iranian desert. They may reach a height of more than 210 meters (700 feet). (*See* **dune.**)

The animals that live in hot deserts (left) and cold deserts (right) have learned to live where there are few plants for food and very little water.

Desert Climates The climates of all deserts are not the same. Deserts closest to the equator are the hottest. The hottest temperature ever recorded on the earth was 58 °C (136° F). This was in the Sahara Desert—in the shade! On a summer day, the temperature in a desert may reach 50° C (120° F) in the sun. The bare soil is even hotter, sometimes reaching 70° C (160° F). But when the sun goes down, the desert cools off quickly. The temperature may fall as much as 30 °C (50° F) during the night.

Deserts far from the equator may be very cold. The largest desert of all is the continent of Antarctica. Most of it is covered with ice, yet it only snows a few inches a year, and only a few plants and animals can live there.

Life in the Desert Low moisture and extreme temperature changes make it difficult to live in a desert. Living things of the desert must have ways to save water. Or they must be able to survive with only a little water. They must also have ways to handle the heat during the day and the cold at night. The kinds of living things that survive in the desert have adapted to its harsh conditions. (*See* **evolution** and **environment.**)

A few kinds of plants are suited to live in the desert. Cacti are common desert plants in the Americas. Instead of leaves, they have thick stems that can store water after a rain. A waxy coating keeps the plants from drying out in the sun. (*See* **cactus.**)

Some trees, such as the mesquite, can live in desert areas where there is water deep underground. The mesquite cannot store water, but its root can grow down nearly 23 meters (75 feet) to reach water.

Some desert plants spend most of their time as seeds. These seeds have a covering that must be washed away before they can sprout. They rest in the soil until rain falls. Then they grow. The new plants make new seeds that lie in the soil until the next rain.

Many mammals, birds, insects, and reptiles are able to live in the desert. Rattlesnakes and horned toads and other lizards live in the North American Desert. They

The kangaroo rat never needs to drink water! A cactus can store water in its spongy stem.

spend their days in the shade, often under rocks, and hunt for food at night. Desert birds, too, are most active at night. Most desert animals get water from the plants or other animals they eat.

One desert animal never drinks water. This animal is the kangaroo rat. It gets its name from its large feet and its habit of hopping from place to place. The kangaroo rat eats only dry seeds. It breaks down this food in its body to make energy. As this happens, the kangaroo rat also produces enough water to stay alive.

The camel is another animal that lives well in the desert. Camels can go for months without water if they have fresh green plants to eat. And they can survive for more than a week with no water at all. A lot of fat is stored in the camel's hump. When the camel is without water, it digests this fat. As fat is changed to energy, enough water is formed to keep the camel alive. (*See* **camel.**)

Most of the year, a desert is quiet and dull to look at. But after a rainfall, the desert comes to life. Shriveled cacti grow plump as they collect water. Bright flowers blossom quickly. Plants spring up where there was only bare soil before. Insects fly about and pollinate the flowers. Then, a few days later, the desert is quiet again, waiting for the next rain.

See also **biome** and **Sahara.**

De Soto, Hernando

Hernando de Soto was a Spanish explorer of the early 1500s. He was probably the first European to see the Mississippi River.

As a young man, De Soto traveled in Central America. Later, he helped Francisco Pizarro conquer the Inca in Peru. (*See* **Inca** and **Pizarro, Francisco.**)

Inca treasures made De Soto rich. He settled in Cuba and became its governor in 1537. He left Cuba when he heard that the mainland to the north (where the United States is today) was full of gold and silver.

In 1539, De Soto landed in Florida with about 600 soldiers. They marched north and then east, but found no gold or silver. De Soto and several others were wounded in fights with the Indians. They could have gone back to Cuba, but De Soto was determined to keep hunting for treasure.

De Soto's party reached the Mississippi River on May 8, 1541. They crossed it and traveled up the Arkansas River. Finally, they turned back to the Mississippi early in 1542. There De Soto died. His men buried him in the river because they did not want the Indians to know he was dead.

See also **Mississippi River.**

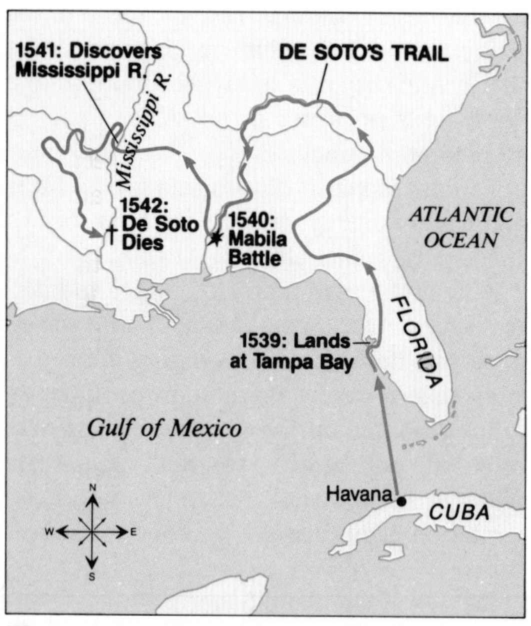

detergent

Every year, people use more than 60 billion pounds (27 billion kilograms) of detergent. They use it to clean clothes, tubs, dishes, pans, metals, and even engine oils. Detergent is a super cleaner.

The word *detergent* has come to mean an artificial cleaner that is not a soap. Soaps are made by combining lye (sodium hydroxide) with fats. Soap may have been made by the ancient Romans, 3,000 years ago. But household detergents were not available in the United States until 1933.

Most detergents are too harsh for your skin. The most common detergent is made from a petroleum product treated with sulfuric acid and lye. Adding acid and lye improves the wetting action of water. The petroleum product helps to dissolve stains and grease. Bleaching agents and brighteners are sometimes added to make laundry whiter. Scrubbing powders for dishwashing may also be part of a detergent.

Some detergents contain phosphorus to improve their cleaning power. But the waste water from these detergents can damage lakes and streams. Laundry detergents no longer contain phosphorus.

See also **bleach** and **soap.**

dew

Dew is the name for tiny drops of water that gather on grass and other plants. It is caused by the same thing that makes small drops form on the outside of a glass of cold liquid on a warm day.

Dew forms when air touches a cold surface. Ordinary air always has some water in it. The water is in the form of a gas, called *water vapor.* Cold air cannot hold as much water vapor as warm air. When the air holds as much water as it can, it has reached its *dew point.* If the air temperature drops below the dew point, the invisible water vapor changes to a liquid. Tiny drops of dew collect. The colder the air becomes, the more

The dew on the flowers and the drops of water on the glass both come from moisture in the air.

dew forms. If the dew point is below freezing, ice crystals form instead of water drops. The ice crystals are called *frost.* (*See* **frost.**)

Dew usually forms at night, when the air and earth cool down. It forms best on clear, windless nights. On clear nights, heat escapes from the atmosphere easily, so the air becomes colder. On overcast nights, clouds hold in the heat. The air stays warmer than on clear nights, and dew may not form. On windy nights, the air keeps moving and does not touch the colder ground for long. It may not cool to the dew point.

diabetes

Diabetes is a disease that keeps some body cells from using sugar. All body cells burn sugar for energy. If diabetes completely stopped cells from using sugar, the cells would die. Diabetes interferes with sugar use by liver, fat, and muscle cells. But sugar use does not stop completely.

When cells cannot burn enough sugar, they send out signals for more. The person feels very hungry. At the same time, sugar is building up in the blood. Water moves out of cells to dilute the sugar in the blood. The hungry cells also release acids. The kidneys work hard to remove the excess sugar, acids, and water. This leads to great thirst and the passing of a lot of urine. If diabetes is not treated, the person loses too much water and soon dies.

A hormone called *insulin* helps cells to burn sugar. Insulin is produced by an organ called the *pancreas.* Diabetes is due either to a lack of insulin or to the inability to use insulin. (*See* **hormone.**)

Some kinds of diabetes are controlled by daily injections of insulin. Other kinds can be controlled by exercise and diet. Scientists are searching for better ways to control diabetes. Someday, they may even find a cure.

diamond

Diamonds are the most prized of all jewels. This is partly because diamonds reflect light brilliantly. It is also partly because diamonds are rare.

A diamond is a crystal made from pure carbon. It is the hardest material known, and it has the highest melting point of any material—3,652° C (6,606° F).

Millions of years ago, high temperatures and pressures deep in the earth turned carbon into diamonds. Liquid rock carried the diamonds to the surface. Most diamonds are mined in South Africa today. In the United States, it is possible to find diamonds in parts of Arkansas.

Above, a natural diamond. Left, the famous Hope diamond. It can be seen at the Smithsonian Institution in Washington, D.C.

Most diamonds are not good enough to be used for jewelry. They may be used to cut rock, glass, steel, and other diamonds. In fact, only a diamond can cut a diamond.

People can make diamonds by putting pure carbon under high temperature and pressure. They are too expensive to sell as jewelry. But scientists have discovered a cheap way of forming a diamond film. This thin, hard layer can be used as a protective coating for drill bits and electronic devices, such as computer chips.

See also **carbon** and **gem.**

Dias, Bartolomeu, *see* explorers

dictator

A dictator is a ruler who has complete control over a country and its people. A dictator often comes to power when a country is troubled and has a weak government. The army often helps the dictator take over. Sometimes, a foreign government helps put a dictator in power.

Once in power, a dictator usually runs a *police state*—a government in which people are controlled by the police and the army. Citizens have few rights. They may be tortured, jailed, or executed without trial. Often, people cannot work or travel where they want to. They are told only what the government wants them to know. Newspapers, radio, and television broadcast *propaganda*—one-sided information that tries to influence the way citizens think.

One of the strongest and most hated dictators of modern times was Joseph Stalin, who ruled the Soviet Union beginning in the 1930s. Another was Adolf Hitler, who controlled Germany at about the same time. (*See* **Stalin, Joseph** and **Hitler, Adolf.**)

Today, dictators rule many countries in Latin America, Africa, and Asia. (*See* **Castro, Fidel.**)

dictionary

A dictionary is a book that gives the spellings and meanings of words. The words are usually listed in alphabetical order. Many dictionaries have other information as well. They show how to pronounce a word and where to separate the syllables. They give the plurals of some nouns. They also give the past tenses of verbs. If there is more than one correct way to spell a word, dictionaries give each one. For example, *cookie* may also be spelled *cooky.*

Many dictionaries also give the history of words. Some include synonyms for each word—other words that mean the same thing. A dictionary will tell you if a word is slang or if it is used in a particular field, such as science or sports.

Some dictionaries are for just one language. For example, an English dictionary tells the meanings of English words in English. Other dictionaries are for two or more languages. A French-English dictionary gives the French words for the English words and the English words for the French.

General dictionaries have words of all kinds. Special dictionaries give words having to do with just one subject. For example, a

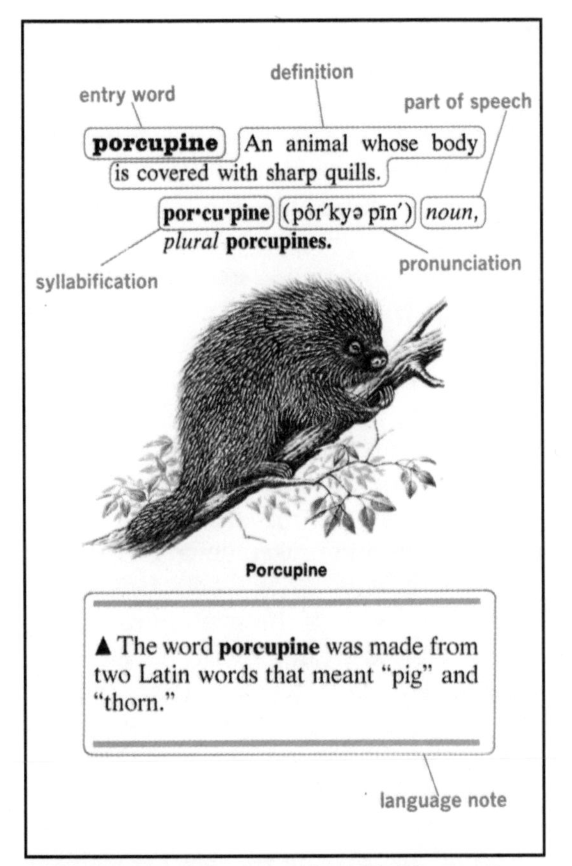

A dictionary gives a word's definition and other useful information.

space dictionary gives meanings of words used for space travel and exploration. A sports dictionary gives meanings of words used in different sports.

Another special kind of dictionary is called a *thesaurus.* It gives synonyms for each word and also *antonyms*—words that have an opposite meaning.

What is a Thesaurus?

A thesaurus is a word book that can give you many *synonyms* for the word you look up – words that have about the same meaning.

For example,

beautiful

attractive	handsome
beauteous	lovely
bonny (Scottish)	pretty
comely	pulchritudinous
fair	stunning
good-looking	

The ancient Greeks and Romans wrote the first dictionaries. They usually listed only difficult words, not everyday words that most people knew.

The first great dictionary of the English language was published in 1755 by Samuel Johnson. He and his helpers studied many books and copied down examples of words in sentences. When Johnson published the dictionary, readers could see just how those words should be used. In 1828, Noah Webster published the first great dictionary of American English. He used many of the same ideas that Samuel Johnson used.

Language is always changing and growing. This is one reason why no dictionary can contain all the words of a language and all their meanings. Dictionary writers keep watching for new words and new ways of using old ones. But these cannot be added to a dictionary that is already on your bookshelf. Some dictionaries are now on computers. It is easier to add new words and meanings to computer dictionaries.

digestion

Digestion is the process by which our bodies break down the food we eat. The digested food can then be used to make energy and help our bodies grow. The *digestive system* is the group of organs in our bodies that digest food. These organs work on the *nutrients* in our food—the carbohydrates, fats, and proteins—so they can be absorbed by the blood stream and carried throughout the body. (*See* **nutrition.**)

Sometimes when you think of food your mouth waters, producing *saliva.* When you eat, saliva mixes with your food. The saliva makes the food moist and easy to swallow. Saliva also contains chemicals called *enzymes* that help start digestion. It is important to chew solid foods well. This breaks the food into small pieces and mixes it with the saliva.

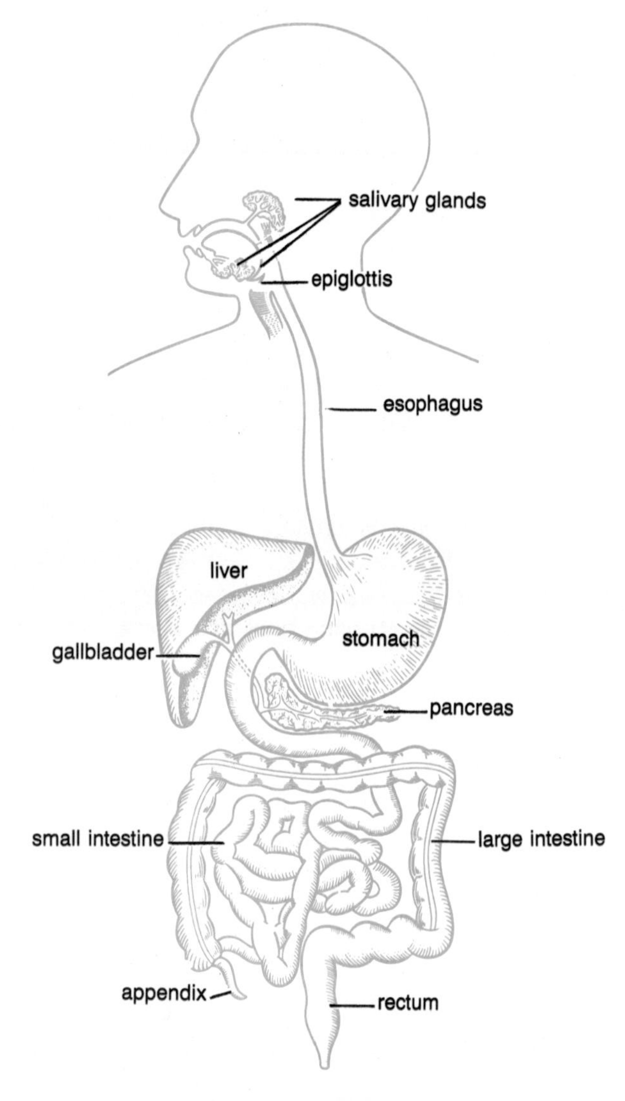

The organs that help digest and use the food we eat make up the digestive system.

From the mouth, the food passes through the throat and into the *esophagus*—the food pipe. When you swallow, a tiny flap of skin called the *epiglottis* closes the windpipe so the food will not go into the lungs. If a small amount of food does get into the windpipe by mistake, your body reacts instantly and causes you to choke the food back out of the windpipe.

The muscles of the esophagus push the food down into the *stomach.* This pouchlike organ in the upper left side of the abdomen can stretch to hold about 3 pints (1.4 liters) of food. The food stays here for several hours, mixing with more enzymes and hydrochloric acid. Gradually, the food dissolves into a liquid. A small muscle at the bottom of the stomach lets the liquid pass out of the stomach a little at a time.

From the stomach, the liquid flows into the *small intestine*—which is not really small. It is about 20 feet (6 meters) long and 1 inch (2.5 centimeters) in diameter. But it fits neatly into a small space because it is coiled up among the other organs in the lower abdomen.

The stomach and the intestine are lined with strong, smooth muscles that gently tighten and then relax to help push the food along its path. As food passes through the small intestine, it is mixed with different digestive juices and broken down further into useful nutrients. These nutrients seep through the walls of the small intestine and into the bloodstream. Blood vessels carry them to all parts of the body. That is how all your body cells receive the nutrients they need to do their jobs.

Some parts of food cannot be digested, such as the fiber from fruits and vegetables. These wastes pass all the way through the small intestine and into the *large intestine.* This organ is wider than the small intestine but not nearly as long. The large intestine absorbs leftover water and minerals, and then passes the solid wastes gradually to the *rectum.* There they are stored until they leave the body through the anus.

Other organs in the abdomen help the body digest food. The *liver,* a large organ in the upper right part of the abdomen, has many jobs. It makes some of the digestive juices that mix with food in the small intestine. The liver also stores some kinds of nutrients and makes new red blood cells.

The *pancreas,* a glandlike organ, produces chemicals that help the body make energy from the sugars and starches in carbohydrates. Many other, smaller glands make enzymes to help process food. (*See* **gland.**)

In a healthy body, digestion is so quiet that we hardly know it is happening. Digestion is very important to good health and is one of the miracles of the human body.

A temporary dike (above) helps protect a house during a flood. Permanent dikes in Holland (left) take new land from the sea.

dikes and levees

People who live near rivers or seas are lucky in many ways. Yet rivers and seas can also be dangerous. The water can rise and flood the land. So people who live nearby build dikes and levees for protection.

Dikes are thick walls built to keep a river or sea from overflowing and flooding low land. In the United States, dikes along riverbanks are usually called *levees.* They may be made of earth, concrete, wood, or sandbags. When a river rises especially high, more sandbags must be piled on top of the levees. More than 3,200 kilometers (2,000 miles) of the Mississippi River are lined with levees.

The most famous dikes are those in the Netherlands. At first, the people built dikes to protect against floods. Later, they used dikes to create new land. A dike is first built in shallow water off the shore. Water on the land side of the dike is pumped out. To get rid of the salt, which kills most plants, the soil is turned over each year for several years. Then the land is ready for farming or building.

See also **flood.**

dinosaur

Dinosaurs lived on Earth many millions of years ago, long before the history of human beings began. No one has ever seen a living dinosaur. But people have found bones, teeth, footprints, and other remains of dinosaurs. These remains tell us about the dinosaurs of long ago.

Dinosaurs lived during the Age of the Reptiles, when the land was warm and swampy. Dinosaurs were reptiles. But, unlike today's reptiles, a dinosaur had legs directly under its body. Today's reptiles—lizards, alligators, and turtles, for example—have legs that stick out from their sides. Many dinosaurs could walk on two legs.

The footprint in this rock was made millions of years ago by a real dinosaur.

Stenonychosaurus is the name of this dinosaur, which was about as tall as an adult human being.

Reptiles of today are cold-blooded—their body temperatures change with the temperature of the environment. Scientists used to think all dinosaurs were cold-blooded, too. But new evidence shows that some dinosaurs may have been warm-blooded. Their temperatures, like ours, may have stayed high even when the environment was cold.

Like the reptiles of today, dinosaurs laid eggs with shells. Fossilized dinosaur nests have been found containing the remains of eggs and baby dinosaurs. Scientists think some dinosaurs cared for their babies for a few months after the young hatched. They brought the young food and protected them from enemies.

There were many kinds of dinosaurs. Some were no larger than chickens. Others were huge. The largest animal that ever walked on land was *Ultrasaurus.* This dinosaur weighed 80 tons and stood as tall as a six-story building.

The name *dinosaur* comes from two Greek words meaning "terrible lizard." Dinosaurs that ate meat were indeed very dangerous. Other dinosaurs ate plants, and some were not really terrible at all.

Meat-Eating Dinosaurs Most meat-eating dinosaurs walked on their large, powerful back legs. The front legs were often small but armed with long, sharp claws for fighting and to hold food. These dinosaurs had huge tails, but when they walked or ran, the tail did not drag on the ground. It stretched out behind, helping the dinosaur keep its balance.

Scientists used to think that all dinosaurs moved slowly compared to mammals. In 1982, some dinosaur tracks were found that showed this was not so. The tracks were made by a meat-eating dinosaur galloping along at 40 kilometers (25 miles) per hour.

Tyrannosaurus was the largest meat-eating dinosaur. It was about 12 meters (40 feet) long, with a large head and a very short neck. It had powerful jaws, and teeth as sharp as knives. It was ferocious!

Some dinosaurs ran away from predators. Others had armor or horns for protection.

Triceratops

Allosaurus and *Ceratosaurus* were other large meat-eaters. They were much like *Tyrannosaurus* in appearance and behavior.

Plant-Eating Dinosaurs Most plant-eating dinosaurs walked on all four legs. The legs were heavy and strong, to support the great weight of the animals. Among the best-known plant-eaters were *Brontosaurus, Ultrasaurus, Brachiosaurus,* and *Diplodocus.* All were among the largest animals that have ever existed on Earth. Each had a small head, a very long neck, and a very long tail. They often lived in groups called *herds.* They moved very slowly, which made it easy for *Allosaurus* and other predators to catch them.

Another group of plant-eaters were the armored dinosaurs. *Stegosaurus* had a row of bony plates sticking up from its back and four long spines near the end of its tail. *Triceratops* had a large bony growth on the back of its head, a long horn on its nose, and a long horn over each eye. It probably used these horns to attack enemies, much as today's rhinoceros uses its horn.

Dinosaur fossils were first discovered in England in 1822. They were the remains of *Iguanodon,* a large dinosaur that walked on its muscular back legs. Its front legs were small, but each hand had a large thumb that looked like a spike. *Iguanodon* probably used its thumbs as weapons.

Why did Dinosaurs Become Extinct? There were dinosaurs on Earth for more than 175 million years. Then, about 65 million years ago, dinosaurs became extinct—died out. Why? Scientists have many theories. Some think the climate changed. Others think that a huge meteorite hit the earth about 65 million years ago. The crash, they say, caused forest fires. So much smoke and dust filled the air that sunlight could not reach the earth's surface. Without sunlight, plants died. Then dinosaurs that ate plants starved to death. Finally, the meat-eating dinosaurs died. The "terrible lizards" were gone.

See also **animals, prehistoric** and **reptile.**

A tornado can lift cars and buildings and set them down hundreds of yards away. The funnel may have winds of 200 miles per hour and cause terrible damage.

disaster

A disaster is a sudden event that causes great damage and affects many people. Many disasters, such as earthquakes and volcanic eruptions, are caused by natural events. One of the first recorded disasters was the great flood described in the Bible. Sometimes a terrible event, such as a famine or a depression, does not happen suddenly. Yet it does cause great hardship and may be called a disaster. (*See* **depression.**)

Many people die from fires and accidents. These disasters are especially terrible because they are often caused by human error and might have been avoided. Some disasters lead to improvements. For example, a terrible fire broke out in Chicago's Iroquois Theater in 1903, killing over 600 people. After that, laws were passed to require more emergency exits in theaters, and scenery that would not burn. In 1942, a fire broke out in a nightclub in Boston. The doors of the nightclub could not be pushed open, and 491 people died. Fire laws now require that all exit doors open outward.

Modern ways of doing things bring disasters that no one could have imagined in the past. In 1984, deadly gas leaked from a chemical factory in Bhopal, India. It killed over 2,000 people and affected as many as 50,000 more.

Natural Disasters Erupting volcanoes shower the earth with lava and hot ashes that can burn, bury, or suffocate people. Vesuvius, a volcano in Italy, erupted in A.D. 79 and killed at least 2,000 people in nearby Pompeii. The city was completely buried. Pompeii's ruins were not discovered for centuries. (*See* **Pompeii.**)

The worst eruption, however, occurred on Krakatoa, a volcanic island in Indonesia. When Krakatoa erupted in 1883, the island was blown apart. A huge tidal wave swept over nearby islands. Dust from the explosion traveled around the world many times before it settled. About 35,000 people were killed.

A volcanic eruption caused great damage to Martinique, an island in the Caribbean Sea. When Mount Pelée erupted there in 1902, all the people in the town of St. Pierre—about 40,000—were killed. The lone survivor from the town was a prisoner. He was saved because he was being held in a dungeon deep under ground.

Earthquakes, too, do tremendous damage. One of the worst hit Lisbon, Portugal, in 1755. It caused terrible fires that destroyed the city. When people ran to the water's edge, many were killed by tidal waves that roared up out of the sea. Altogether, 60,000 people lost their lives.

Even worse was the Japanese earthquake of 1923. It destroyed the whole city of Yokohama and half of Tokyo. As many as 200,000 people may have been lost.

An earthquake in China was reported to have killed 800,000 people in the 1500s. In

1973, another earthquake in China killed over 240,000.

The worst flood in history also happened in China. The Huang He (Yellow River) overflowed its banks in 1887. The flooding was so great that the water completely covered 11 cities. People fled waves as high as 30 feet (9 meters). This terrible flood probably killed at least 900,000 Chinese.

Fires Fires can destroy cities and vast amounts of land. The Great Fire of London, in 1666, burned for five days and ruined most of the city. More than 13,000 houses burned to the ground, but only 6 people lost their lives.

Another great fire swept the city of Chicago, Illinois in 1871. It started in a barn and quickly spread. Most houses at that time were made of wood, and no rain had fallen in the area for 14 weeks. The fire destroyed an area of 3½ square miles (9 square kilometers). A third of Chicago's people were left homeless by the fire.

Ships and Aircraft The ocean liner *Titanic* was the fastest ship afloat and supposedly unsinkable. But when it hit an iceberg on its first voyage, in 1912, it sank in a few hours. Only 704 of its 2,207 passengers and crew members escaped.

The *Hindenburg* was a *dirigible*— airship. In 1937, a crowd gathered to watch it land in Lakehurst, New Jersey. The airship, which was filled with hydrogen gas, suddenly burst into flames and exploded before their eyes. Thirty-six people died.

The worst single disaster in the history of air travel occurred not in the air but on the ground, in 1977. Two jumbo jets collided on a runway in the Canary Islands. A total of 581 people lost their lives.

A fire swept Chicago in 1871. It destroyed most of the central and northern parts of the city. A new, modern city replaced the ruins.

When famine strikes, there is widespread starvation and suffering.

A shocking air disaster horrified millions of television viewers in 1986. The space shuttle *Challenger* caught fire and exploded shortly after lift-off from Cape Canaveral. All seven astronauts aboard—including the first schoolteacher who was to go into space—lost their lives.

Some disasters seem unavoidable, because there is no way of telling that they will happen. Yet scientists have found ways to predict many natural events and keep them from becoming disasters. We can prevent some disasters—natural and man-made—by being careful and thinking ahead.

See also **avalanche; earthquake; fire; flood; hurricane; landslide; volcano;** and **weather.**

disease and sickness

Disease is sickness of the body or mind. Some diseases are caused by poor diet, smoking, air pollution, alcohol, stress, worry, birth defects, or simply growing old. These are called *noninfectious* diseases.

In the 1800s, Louis Pasteur and other scientists discovered that many diseases are caused by tiny living organisms, commonly called *germs.* Germs that cause disease include bacteria, viruses, protists, and fungi. Diseases caused by germs are called *infectious diseases.* (*See* **Pasteur, Louis.**)

Most infectious diseases can be spread from one person to another. Some spread through the air when a person coughs or sneezes. Others can be spread through food or water. (*See* **chicken pox; influenza; measles; mumps; polio;** and **smallpox.**)

Some of the most deadly infectious diseases are spread by insects that feed on blood. Mosquitoes can spread malaria and yellow fever this way. (*See* **malaria; plague;** and **Reed, Walter.**)

AIDS is a serious illness caused by a tiny virus. It was first recognized in 1981. It damages the body's disease-fighting system. People with AIDS get many other infectious diseases because their bodies can't fight them off.

In the United States today, noninfectious diseases such as cardiovascular disease, cancer, diabetes, and asthma are now the leading causes of death. These diseases often take a long time to develop.

Cardiovascular diseases affect the heart and blood vessels, causing high blood pressure, heart attacks, and strokes. (*See* **heart disease.**)

Cancer occurs when certain cells of the body multiply too rapidly. Diabetes is caused by lack of the hormone insulin, or by the body's inability to use the insulin it has. (*See* **cancer** and **diabetes.**)

Many diseases can be prevented. You can do this by practicing good health habits. It is important to eat a balanced diet and to get plenty of rest and exercise. People can also protect their health by not smoking and by avoiding alcohol and other drugs unless prescribed by a doctor. Regular medical checkups are important, too. A doctor may be able to detect a disease in its early stages, when it is easiest to treat and cure.

Mental illnesses may result from physical disorders, such as birth defects or brain injuries, or from a variety of other causes. Psychiatrists and psychologists are doctors who specialize in mental illnesses.

See also **allergy; antibody;** and **drugs and medicines.**

Above, Walt Disney and some of the well-loved characters he created—Goofy, Uncle Scrooge, Pluto, Donald Duck, Mickey Mouse, and Tinkerbell, the fairy. Right, Disney World in Florida, a Disney theme park offering fun for all. Other Disney parks are in California and Japan.

Disney, Walt

Walt Disney died in 1966, but millions of people around the world will never forget him. He created dozens of colorful, amusing characters, including the famous Mickey Mouse and Donald Duck. You have probably seen his movies and TV shows, or maybe you have visited Disneyland or Disney World.

Walter E. Disney was born in Chicago in 1901 but grew up in Kansas City, Missouri. When he was 19 years old, he got a job making cartoon advertisements. In the 1920s, he started working on a new kind of movie. He used *animation*—a way of showing a series of drawings in order very quickly, so that characters seem to move before your eyes. (*See* **cartoon, animated.**)

In 1928, Walt Disney made a short animated film—a *cartoon*—about a mouse named Mickey. It was so successful that he made many more. In 1937, he made the first movie-length cartoon, *Snow White and the Seven Dwarfs*. Others followed, including *Fantasia, Bambi,* and *Cinderella*. Disney's company also made movies with live actors, such as *Treasure Island* and *Mary Poppins*.

In the 1950s, Disney built a theme park called Disneyland in California. Visitors could enjoy exhibits, shows, rides, and characters from his movies. Later, Disney World and Epcot Center opened in Florida. Every year, more than 30 million people from around the world visit these parks.

See also **theme park.**

District of Columbia

The District of Columbia is the area where Washington, the capital of the United States, is located. It is a triangular region of 69 square miles (179 square kilometers) between Maryland and Virginia.

During the early years of the United States, Congress met in several cities, including New York and Philadelphia. In 1783, Congress decided that there should be a permanent capital. Leaders from North and South argued over where it should be.

In 1790, Secretary of the Treasury Alexander Hamilton suggested that the capital be built on land given to the federal government. President George Washington was asked to pick the exact location. Maryland and Virginia donated land for the new capital. The city of Washington was built on the land given by Maryland. The land donated by Virginia was later returned to that state.

The District is ruled by the federal government. It is not a state and has no voting representatives in Congress. The people do elect their own mayor and city council. But the federal government still has the power to make the final decisions.

See also **Washington, D.C.**

diving

When you hear the word *diving,* the first thing that comes to mind may be the fun of diving into a neighborhood pool on a hot summer day. You may also think of *scuba diving,* diving to explore the world beneath the sea. Or you may think of *competitive diving,* complicated twists and turns done in the air when diving into a pool.

Competitive diving is an Olympic sport. There are two kinds of competitive diving. One is called *springboard diving.* The other is *platform diving.* Springboard divers jump from the same kind of diving board you see at a local pool. The board is bouncy, helping divers to jump high into the air before diving into the pool. Platform divers jump from a firm surface—usually nearly 33 feet (10 meters) above the water. Competitors in both kinds of diving do somersaults and twists in the air before entering the water.

(Caution: These dives are very dangerous. Do not try to do dives that involve twists and turns without special training!)

A group of judges rates each diver's performance. Olympic divers are judged on how well they do in a series of ten dives. One diver you may have heard of is Greg Louganis. He won two gold medals, one for springboard and one for platform diving, at the 1984 Summer Olympics.

Scuba diving is not a competitive sport, but it is an exciting pastime. Scuba divers spend long periods of time underwater. They breathe through hoses connected to air-filled tanks on their backs. They see through clear plastic masks over their faces. The term *scuba* comes from all this breathing equipment. The letters stand for *self-contained underwater breathing apparatus.*

Scuba divers swim among schools of fish and see unusual underwater plants. It is fun, but before going scuba diving, you must learn how to do it from a licensed instructor.

Diving may mean jumping off a board (below) or exploring underwater (right).
On next page, a diver does an inward pike. He begins the dive facing the board.

1.

2.

3.

4.

5.

Another kind of diving is *skydiving.* Sky divers do not jump into the water. Instead, they jump into the air from an airplane! Before opening their parachutes, they glide like birds on currents of air. This kind of diving, too, requires special training by licensed and experienced instructors.

division, *see* arithmetic

divorce

Divorce is the legal step that ends a marriage. A divorce agreement states that a man and a woman are no longer husband and wife. It also may explain how their property is to be divided and who should care for their children.

In the United States, divorce laws differ from state to state. In some states, a husband or wife must go to court and tell why the marriage has ended. Sometimes they must prove that the other partner has done something wrong. Other states have *no-fault* divorce laws. This means that the husband and wife can simply tell the court that they cannot solve certain problems in their marriage. Neither one needs to claim that the other did something wrong.

Sometimes divorce agreements require one partner to pay *alimony*—a certain amount of money paid to the other, usually every month. In the past, few married women worked outside the home. They were busy keeping house and raising children. After a divorce, they needed help to support themselves. The court required the former husbands to pay alimony. Today, few divorces provide for payment of alimony.

Divorce agreements do provide for the couple's children. Usually one parent is given *custody* of the children. This means that the children live with that parent.

The parent who does not have custody often pays *child support*—a certain amount of money given each month to help pay for clothing, food, housing, and other expenses.

This parent also has *visitation rights.* This means that he or she may visit the children, or have the children come to visit, on weekends, during summers, or at other particular times.

Sometimes custody of a child is awarded to both parents. This is called *joint custody.* In these cases, the child may live part of the time with each parent.

Getting a divorce is often an unhappy experience for the couple and for their children. Usually this unhappiness becomes less as time passes. Many divorced people eventually find new partners. Children of the first marriage then have a stepmother or stepfather as well as their own mother and father. If the new partner already has children too, the children will be stepsisters and stepbrothers. This may take some getting used to, but can work out very happily.

See also **marriage.**

Djibouti, *see* Africa

DNA

Every cell in your body works to carry out a special job to keep you alive. Your cells work all the time and you do not even have to think about it. How can this happen? The answer is in a chemical called DNA. These three letters are a short way to say *deoxyribonucleic acid.*

DNA is found in almost every cell of every living thing. You can look into the nucleus at the center of a plant cell or animal cell with a very powerful microscope. There you can see tiny threads, called *chromosomes.* These threads are mostly DNA. If you magnify the DNA even more, you will see that it is shaped like a very thin ladder. But this ladder is not straight at all—it is twisted, like a spring or corkscrew.

DNA is an important part of all living things. It is a complete set of instructions for your body cells, telling them everything they must do to keep you alive. It tells offspring how to be like their parents. It tells cells how to repair themselves. It tells them how to grow. It also tells them how to make the different substances you need to stay healthy. DNA can even tell cells how to cooperate—work together.

The instructions in a thread of DNA are not read all at once. Instead, just a single piece or a few pieces of information are read. Each piece of information in DNA is a section of the DNA ladder. The sections are called *genes.*

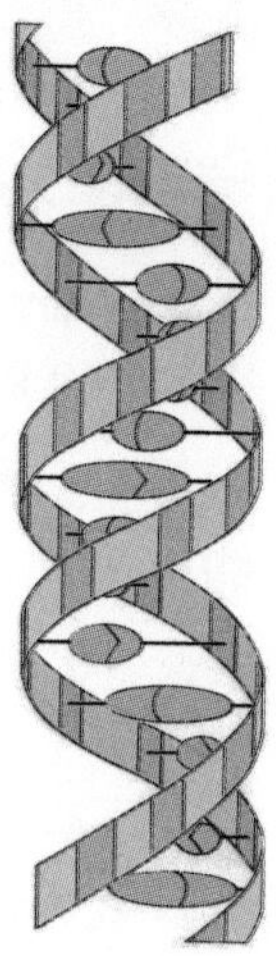

A DNA molecule is shaped like a ladder. The ladder's sides twist around each other. The steps of the ladder are chemicals that make a code. The code can give instructions to a cell.

The DNA cannot leave the nucleus of a cell. So how does it direct a cell to work? The answer is in another chemical. This chemical is called RNA, short for *ribonucleic acid.* RNA can leave the nucleus. It takes instructions from one or a few genes in the nucleus and carries this information to the other parts of the cell. You might think of DNA as a book of instructions. The RNA reads those instructions and explains them to the rest of the cell. The cell carries out the instructions to keep itself—and you—alive and healthy.

The instructions carried by the DNA are different in different living things. The DNA in a bacterium tells it how to be a bacterium. The DNA in a rose tells it how to be a rose. And the DNA in a jellyfish tells it how to be a jellyfish. Each kind of living thing has its own special DNA instructions.

See also **cell; genetics;** and **heredity.**

doctor, *see* medicine

dog

Thousands of years ago, there were no pet dogs. There only were wild dogs. But people soon domesticated—tamed—some of the dogs. In fact, dogs were the first animals tamed by man. Dogs and people have been friends ever since. Dogs live everywhere people live, from the Arctic to the tropics.

Dogs are faithful and devoted companions. They may also do important jobs. Some herd sheep and cattle and protect them from wolves. Others are used as watchdogs. St. Bernards can find people buried by avalanches. German shepherds and other breeds are trained to be guide dogs—dogs that lead people who are blind.

Dogs come in many sizes, shapes, and colors. But they all have five toes on their front feet and four on their back feet. They are all meat-eaters.

A dog's body is covered with a coat of hair. Some breeds have short hair, others have long hair. Some have straight hair, others have curly hair. The Mexican hairless dog has almost no hair at all.

Dogs can hear much better than we can, and they have an excellent sense of smell. Their eyesight is about as good as ours, but they probably do not see colors, just shades of black, gray, and white.

Dogs are intelligent animals. They can be trained to do tricks and to behave properly. Dog owners train their dogs to obey commands such as "Sit," "Stay," and "Come." This makes it easier to control their dogs.

Dog Behavior Dogs communicate in many ways. They make different sounds, each sound having its own meaning. Growls and some barks mean "Go away." Other barks say "I'm so happy to see you!"

Dogs communicate with their bodies, too. A wagging tail is usually a friendly gesture. A tail held stiffly over the animal's back says "Keep away!" When a dog is afraid, it may flatten its ears against its head and curl its tail down between its rear legs. When it is angry, its ears and hair stand straight up.

Territory—the area in which a dog lives—is very important to a dog. The dog marks its territory with urine and special scents. These scents are different from those of all other dogs. The dog can recognize its own scent. It also learns to recognize the scents of other dogs that live nearby. When a dog wanders away from home, it lays down a trail of scent. It can follow this trail to find its way home.

Dogs like this German shepherd can be trained to be guides for blind people.

Some dogs learn quickly to catch a ball or a Frisbee and carry it back to their master.

Like small children, these beagle puppies love to run and play.

Puppies Puppies—young dogs—are completely helpless when they are born. They cannot see or hear. They depend on their mother for all their needs. The mother feeds and cleans them. She keeps them warm. She carries them home if they wander off.

A puppy's eyes open when it is about two weeks old. When it is three weeks old, it begins to walk. At four weeks, it starts to play with its brothers and sisters. They wrestle and chase one another. Like children, puppies need lots of love and attention.

Dog Breeds The American Kennel Club (AKC) lists 128 different breeds of dogs. The smallest is the Chihuahua, which may weigh less than 2 kilograms (4 pounds). The St. Bernard is the heaviest—it may weigh more than 90 kilograms (200 pounds).

When two dogs of the same breed mate, they produce purebred puppies that grow up to look very much like their parents. When dogs of two different breeds mate, the puppies may look very different from either parent, and from one another. Most dogs are a mixture of breeds.

Some hunting dogs "point" to birds, helping hunters to find the birds.

The American Kennel Club groups dogs in seven main categories: sporting dogs, hounds, working dogs, terriers, toy dogs, nonsporting dogs, and herding dogs.

Sporting dogs help people who hunt with guns. These breeds include spaniels, setters, pointers, and retrievers.

Hounds also help people hunt. Some, such as Afghans and greyhounds, rely on their eyes and their speed. Others, such as beagles and bloodhounds, hunt by scent.

Terriers are good at getting foxes and other animals out of their underground homes. A terrier may even follow its prey into the underground tunnels of their dens.

Working dogs and herding dogs were developed to pull sleds, act as guards, and herd animals. They include collies, boxers, sheepdogs, and St. Bernards.

Big and small: A collie can weigh as much as 75 pounds (34 kilograms), and a dachshund as little as 5 pounds (2 kilograms).

Toy dogs are very small. They are often called "lapdogs" because they are small enough to fit on a person's lap. Among them are Chihuahuas, Pekingese, and toy poodles.

Nonsporting breeds include poodles, dalmatians, and bulldogs. Most of these used to be working or sporting breeds. Now they are mostly household pets.

There are hundreds of dog shows in the United States each year. The most important is the Westminster Kennel Club show in New York City every February. Judges rate each purebred dog on its appearance and performance. The best example of each breed is chosen, and then the best dog in the entire show.

See also **dog family** and **pets.**

dog family

The dogs people keep as pets have relatives that live in the wild. Wolves, foxes, and coyotes are familiar members of the dog family. Other family members—such as jackals, dingoes, and dholes—are not as well known.

All dogs are carnivores—meat-eaters. Their bodies are designed for hunting. Dogs have an excellent sense of smell and hearing. They have powerful jaws and sharp teeth. They have strong legs and feet. They may not run as fast as their prey, but they can run for a long time. They wear out the prey in a long chase.

Foxes and some others hunt alone. Dingoes and wolves hunt in groups called *packs.* Some packs are very large. The African hunting dog may hunt in packs of up to 60 animals. The packs can capture antelope and other large prey. These hunting dogs are not as closely related to pet dogs as wolves and dingoes are.

Wild dogs make various sounds to communicate with one another. They may bark, growl, yelp, or whine. The cries of wolves and jackals include long howls. Coyotes and African hunting dogs have almost musical "songs."

Many wild dogs are thought to mate for life. They are very good parents. Both father and mother help to raise the pups.

The dog family includes about 40 kinds of animals. The smallest is the fennec fox, which lives in desert regions of northern Africa and the Middle East. It weighs only 1.4 kilograms (3 pounds). The largest is the gray wolf of North America, Europe, and Asia. It may weigh 80 kilograms (175 pounds).

Jackals live in Africa and Asia. They look like a cross between a fox and a wolf. They usually hunt alone or in pairs and will eat almost anything.

The dingo is the only wild member of the dog family found in Australia. It is also the only large mammal in Australia that is not a marsupial—an animal with a pouch in which to carry its young. The dingo is about the size of a collie.

Another interesting member of this family is the dhole, which lives in the mountains of central and eastern Asia. It is a bit larger than a coyote and looks like a dog, except for its rounded ears. Unlike most of the dog family, the dhole does not dig. It lives in burrows made by other animals, or in caves, or in holes in a rocky ledge.

See also **dog; coyote; fox;** and **wolf.**

Below, a pair of jackals. Left, a wild dog from Tanzania, in Africa. These members of the dog family live by hunting.

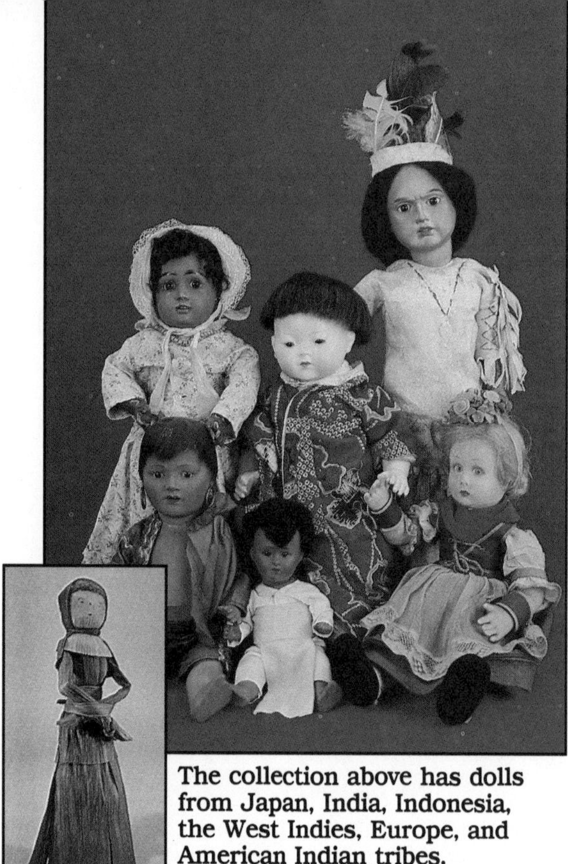

The collection above has dolls from Japan, India, Indonesia, the West Indies, Europe, and American Indian tribes. At left is a cornhusk doll.

doll

A doll is a small figure that resembles a person. Dolls are among the most beloved of all toys. You may even think of them as friends. But the first dolls were not meant to be played with.

Historians say that dolls were made of clay, wood, or bone more than 40,000 years ago, and used in religious ceremonies.

During the 1300s and 1400s in Europe, dolls were used as little fashion models. Clothesmakers dressed dolls up in the latest fashions and showed them to customers.

Soon, people realized that dolls could also be wonderful toys. By the 1800s, dolls had become big business. Dollmakers in many countries worked to create fancier, more unusual dolls from wood, cloth, china, paper, or wax. France and Germany were the leading producers of dolls. In 1824, a clever German inventor figured out how to make a doll say "Mama."

Some dolls have remained favorites, year after year. Raggedy Ann, first introduced in the early 1900s, is still popular today. So is Barbie, introduced in 1959. Like the old European fashion dolls, Barbie has many sets of stylish clothes.

Costume dolls—dolls wearing traditional dress of nations around the world—have always been favorites with collectors.

dolphins and porpoises

Dolphins and porpoises live in water and are excellent swimmers. But they are not fish. They are mammals closely related to whales. Like all mammals, they breathe through lungs. They must come to the water's surface for air. A nostril called a *blowhole* on top of the animal's head allows it to breathe air even while swimming at top speed.

Like whales, dolphins and porpoises can produce high-pitched sounds. They use certain sounds to signal one another. Other sounds are often used to find food by

An easy way to tell a porpoise from a dolphin is by the shape of its snout. The porpoise's snout is rounded, while the dolphin's is more pointed.

echolocation, much as bats do. The sounds produced by the animal bounce off objects in the water and return as echoes. When the animal hears the echo, it learns the position and size of objects in its path.

Dolphins and porpoises do not have external—outer—ears like ours. Their ears are internal, but much more sensitive. They can hear sounds we cannot.

A dolphin or porpoise has a streamlined body that moves easily through the water. It has two flippers and a powerful tail. At the end of the tail are fins called *flukes.* The animal uses its flukes to swim. The flukes move up and down, unlike a fish's tail, which moves from side to side. Some dolphins can swim at speeds up to 36 kilometers (23 miles) per hour.

There are about 50 known kinds of dolphins and porpoises. A few live in fresh water, but most live in the ocean. Most dolphins are slender, with pointed snouts. Porpoises have heavier bodies and rounded snouts. Both animals usually live in groups called *herds.* There may be hundreds of animals in a herd. They feed on sardines, herring, and other fish. They also like squid.

The dolphins you probably know best are the bottle-nosed dolphins. They have dark gray backs, white or pale gray bellies, and may be 4 meters (12 feet) long. Bottle-nosed dolphins are popular entertainers at aquariums and marinelands. They are playful, friendly, and very intelligent. People have trained them to catch balls, jump through hoops, and perform other tricks. Dolphins have been known to rescue other dolphins and even human swimmers by swimming beneath them and holding them up.

The most familiar porpoise is the common porpoise. It lives along coasts, but often swims up rivers and into harbors. It is about 1.5 meters (5 feet) long, with a black back and white belly. Some are all black.

See also **mammal** and **whale.**

Dominica, *see* West Indies

Dominican Republic

Capital: Santo Domingo
Area: 18,816 square miles (48,733 square kilometers)
Population (1985): about 6,614,000
Official language: Spanish

The Dominican Republic is a small country that shares the island of Hispaniola with Haiti. Hispaniola lies between Cuba and Puerto Rico in the Caribbean Sea. It is part of a group of islands called the West Indies. (*See* **West Indies.**)

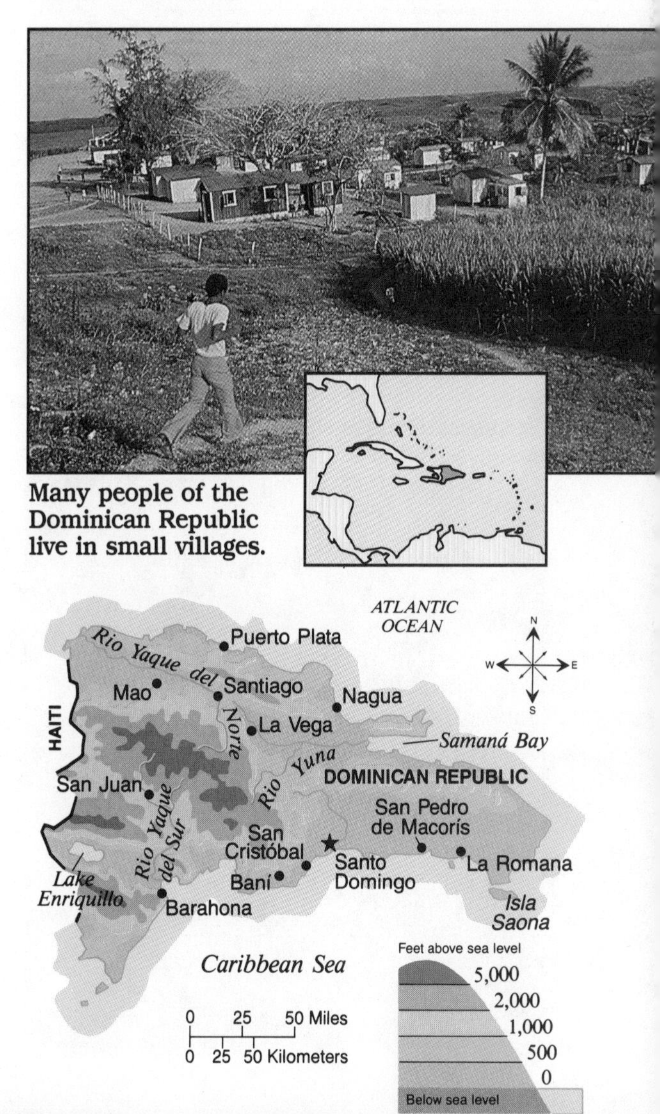

Many people of the Dominican Republic live in small villages.

Christopher Columbus landed on Hispaniola in 1492, on his first voyage to the New World. His brother, Bartholomeo, founded the town of Santo Domingo. Today, Santo Domingo is a busy seaport. It is also the Dominican Republic's capital and largest city.

Most Dominicans live in small villages. They own small farms or work on large plantations raising sugarcane, bananas, coffee, cacao, or other crops. Some Dominicans mine bauxite, a mineral used to make aluminum. People in the cities usually work as fishermen or in factories.

At times, the Dominican Republic has been ruled by harsh dictators or other countries. Twice in the 1900s, U.S. soldiers were sent there to keep peace.

Douglass, Frederick

Frederick Douglass was a leader in the fight against slavery in the United States, from the middle to the end of the 1800s.

Douglass was born a slave in Tuckahoe, Maryland, around 1818. His master's wife taught him to read. Her husband objected to the lessons and punished Douglass harshly. Douglass ran away to Massachusetts in 1838. In 1841, he spoke out against slavery at a meeting of the Massachusetts Antislavery Society. Many of his listeners were moved by his accounts of life as a slave. They encouraged him to continue making speeches against slavery. In 1845, Douglass published the story of his life, *Narrative of the Life of Frederick Douglass.*

Frederick Douglass fought to end slavery and gain rights for black people.

Douglass started an antislavery newspaper, the *North Star,* in 1847. When the Civil War began, he organized two regiments of black soldiers to fight in the Union Army.

When the Civil War ended, slaves were freed, but most blacks were still treated unfairly. Douglass continued to speak out for the rights of blacks. He died in Washington, D.C., in 1895.

See also **slavery** and **Civil War.**

dove, *see* pigeons and doves

dragon

People long ago told stories about monster reptiles that breathed fire and could swallow a ship in one gulp. According to legend, some of these dragons could even fly. They lived in caves or in the sea, and often guarded treasures. People thought dragons looked something like dinosaurs. But the people who made up these stories lived millions of years after the last dinosaurs died and knew nothing about them.

One tale tells how the ancient hero Beowulf fought such a dragon. The dragon didn't start the fight. It found a treasure and took to sleeping on it. Then, one day, while the dragon slept, a man stole a tiny gold cup from the treasure. As soon as the dragon awoke, it knew the cup was missing. The dragon swooped down on the nearest town and burned it with his breath. Beowulf went out to fight the dragon, and they killed each other. (*See* **English writers.**)

Another dragon who guards treasure appears in *The Hobbit* by J.R.R. Tolkien. This dragon stole the treasure from hardworking dwarfs, who eventually got it back.

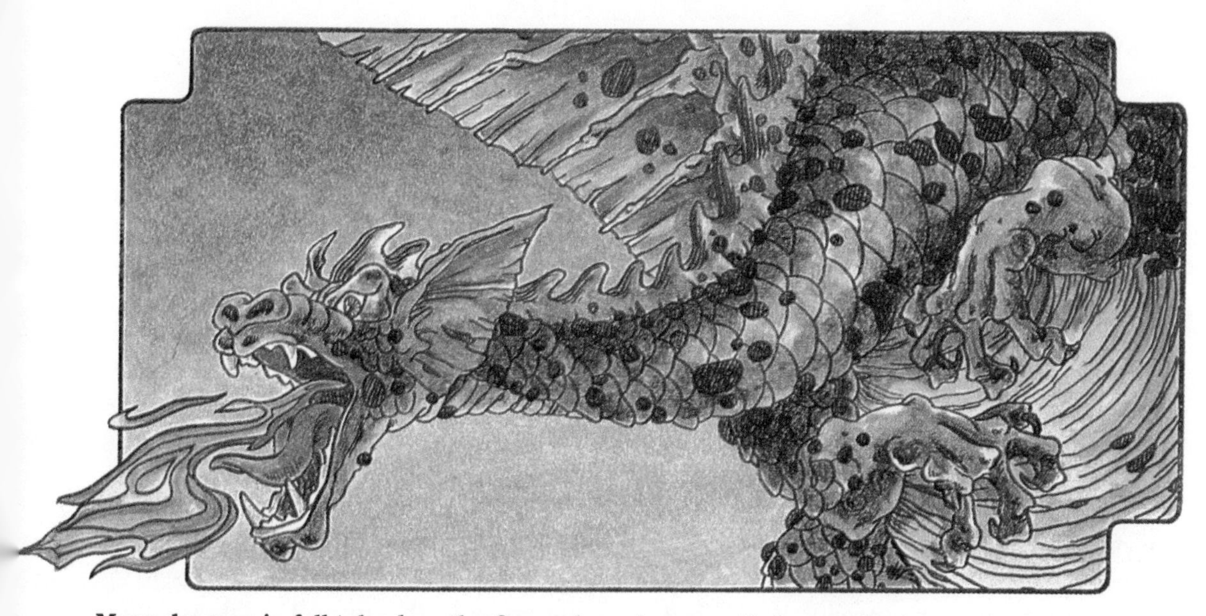

Many dragons in folktales breathe fire and can burn up their enemies.

In many storybooks, a princess is carried off by a dragon. The hero who saves such an unfortunate princess gets to marry her. This is just what happened to the princess Andromeda. Luckily for her, the Greek hero Perseus happened to pass by, saw that she was in danger, and saved her.

In stories about the Middle Ages in Europe, knights who wanted to prove their courage had to kill a dragon. Rescuing a lady at the same time was a double good deed. The most famous dragon-slayer was Saint George, England's patron saint. He slew a dragon with his magic sword and saved a fair maiden.

Artists have often painted saints standing on dragons. This is because in the Western world, dragons represent evil. If the saint is standing on a dragon, it shows that the saint has conquered evil.

But not all people consider dragons evil. The Chinese think that dragons bring good luck, and the dragon is the national symbol of China.

Drake, Sir Francis

Sir Francis Drake, an English seaman of the 1500s, was both an explorer and a pirate. He was the second person ever to sail around the world (Magellan was first), and the first Englishman to do it. Drake's victory over Spanish warships in 1588 made England the ruler of the seas.

Drake was the most famous of the English *sea dogs*—daring sea captains who robbed Spanish ships. England's Queen Elizabeth I gave them ships and money for their voyages. In return, the sea dogs gave the queen much of the Spanish gold and other treasure they stole. England and Spain were enemies, so the English treated Drake and the other sea dogs as heroes rather than as pirates.

Drake's voyage around the world lasted from 1577 to 1580. He sailed from England to the tip of South America, then north to San Francisco Bay in North America. From there, he crossed the Pacific Ocean and eventually returned to England. Drake's trip helped open the Pacific Ocean to British trade.

In 1588, Drake's ships defeated the Invincible Armada, a powerful fleet of ships sent by Spain to invade England. Drake died in 1596, when he was on his way home from the West Indies.

See also **English history** and **Elizabeth I.**

drama, *see* play; actors and acting

dream, *see* sleep

drugs and medicines

Drugs are chemical substances that can change the way our bodies work. When drugs are used to help people feel better, they are called medicines. Some medicines kill the tiny creatures that cause infections. Others can reduce pain or coughing, so that a sick person can rest more easily. Still other medicines help the body work better so that it will feel better.

When people get sick and visit the doctor, the doctor may send them to a *pharmacy* —drug store—to get medicine. Often, the doctor writes out a message called a *prescription* on a small sheet of paper. The prescription tells what kind of medicine the sick person needs and how often the medicine should be taken. At the drug store, a *pharmacist*—person licensed to fill prescriptions—prepares the medicine and gives it to the sick person.

Drugs and medicines come in many forms. Some are pills to be swallowed. Some are liquids to be swallowed a spoonful at a time. Some medicines come in the form of liquids for spreading on cuts, scratches, or rashes. There are also ointments or creams for rubbing on sore muscles.

Some mild medicines are on the shelves in drug stores and supermarkets. They are also advertised on television, and in magazines, newspapers, and other places. People can buy them without a doctor's prescription. Stronger medicines can be sold only if a doctor writes a prescription.

Drugs That Fight Infection Antibiotics are drugs that kill bacteria. They are used to fight infections and illnesses that are caused by bacteria. Bacteria cause many ear infections, for example. So if you have ever had an earache, you may have taken an antibiotic. (*See* **antibiotic.**)

Antibiotics are usually taken by mouth. They enter the bloodstream and are carried to the place where the infection is. There are many drugs in the antibiotic family. One of the most famous antibiotics is penicillin. (*See* **penicillin.**)

Reducing Pain The most common medicines in the United States are those that soothe small aches and pains. For many years, nearly all painkilling medicines contained aspirin. Many still do. Aspirin can also help reduce fever and swelling.

Another drug, acetominophen, is now nearly as popular as aspirin for reducing pain. It is sold under many brand names and is often advertised. Still another painkiller, ibuprofen, is also widely used.

For severe pain, doctors sometimes have their patient take very strong painkillers called *narcotics.* These drugs can be very helpful for people with serious illnesses.

WHAT IS A PHARMACIST?

A pharmacist is trained to prepare and sell drugs and medicines. He or she usually works in a *pharmacy* — a drugstore. The pharmacist receives a *prescription* from a doctor. It tells what kind of medicine should be prepared, how much, and how the patient should use it. The pharmacist puts the medicine in a container and labels it. The label tells the name of the patient, the name of the medicine, and the doctor's directions for use.

But they are also very dangerous, because they are *addictive.* This means that people can begin to depend on the drug, and will want it even if they are not sick. In fact, they will most likely get sick if they stop using it. For this reason, it is against the law to sell narcotics without a doctor's prescription. (*See* **addiction.**)

Anesthetics are used to prevent severe pain. A *general anesthetic* causes a person to "go to sleep," or lose consciousness. It is used for a person who is about to have a major operation. A *local anesthetic* makes a particular part of the body numb. Dentists sometimes use local anesthetics to make part of a person's mouth numb before doing dental work. The numbness wears off after a little while. (*See* **anesthetic.**)

Helping the Body Work Many drugs do their job by either increasing or decreasing some body function.

Some people get stomachaches—also called "heartburn"—because their stomachs make too much stomach acid. Medicines can reduce the amount of acid in the stomach and relieve the pain. There are also medicines for many other ailments of the digestive system.

Many illnesses affect breathing. Some cold medicines can clear up a stuffy head during a cold. Others help reduce coughing. There are also medicines for long-lasting illnesses that affect breathing, such as allergies and asthma. These medicines help clear the passages to the lungs. A doctor must prescribe many of these medicines, because they are very strong.

Many illnesses affect the heart and the circulation of the blood. People with these illnesses often take *cardiovascular* drugs. Some of these can control an unsteady heartbeat. Others make the heartbeat stronger. Still others lower blood pressure. (*See* **heart disease.**)

Some people lack certain *hormones* —chemicals made by glands in the body. Hormones control many different body functions. People who lack hormones must take

KINDS OF MEDICINE

This table gives types of medicine that people use for minor illnesses.

CAUTION: DO NOT TAKE ANY MEDICINE UNLESS YOU ARE GIVEN IT BY A PARENT OR OTHER ADULT.

Name	Purpose
analgesic	to relieve headache or minor aches and pains
cough medicine	to reduce coughing, soothe sore throat
antihistamine	to relieve sneezing, runny nose, itchy eyes
decongestant	to clear stuffy head
antacid	to relieve indigestion, heartburn
antiseptic	to clean small cuts and scratches, reduce chances of infection

them in the form of pills or injections.

People who have diabetes either lack the hormone insulin, or cannot use the insulin they produce effectively. They must regularly receive insulin injections. Hormones are also used in birth-control pills. (*See* **diabetes** and **reproduction.**)

Medicines That Affect the Brain Some people have trouble sleeping. There are many kinds of sleeping medicines. Some are mild. Others are very strong and may cause addiction if used all the time. Sleeping medicines affect the brain.

Other people are too sleepy. They may use a *stimulant* drug to make them feel wide awake. The caffeine in coffee and colas is a mild stimulant. Strong stimulants, such as cocaine, can be very dangerous.

Some people feel very anxious and nervous all the time. For such people, there are drugs called *tranquilizers.* These drugs can help people feel calm without making them feel sleepy. Tranquilizers must be prescribed by a doctor.

Cancer and the Immune System Many drugs are used to combat cancer. These drugs attack and kill cancer cells, but also hurt normal cells. Scientists are hoping to develop drugs that will kill only cancer cells. (*See* **cancer.**)

Sometimes, a body organ is so badly damaged by disease or accident that it cannot be repaired. In that case, an organ from another person may be transplanted into the patient. The patient's immune system will try to destroy the "foreign" tissue. So the patient must take drugs that weaken the immune system. Often, people who receive transplants must take such drugs for the rest of their lives. (*See* **transplant.**)

Skin Problems Medicines for skin problems are often in the form of ointments or creams. Some skin infections are caused by bacteria. These can be treated with antibiotic ointments. Skin can also be infected by a fungus. One common fungus infection is called *athlete's foot.* There are medicines that can kill fungi and end these infections. People with some skin problems use hormonelike drugs called *steroids* that help promote healing.

Drug Safety *All drugs and medicines can be dangerous if not used properly.* They should always be kept out of the reach of small children. They should also be kept in labeled containers so that no one will take the wrong medicine by mistake.

Many drugs have *side effects.* For example, cold medicines that clear up your stuffy head can also make you sleepy. Some medicines can also harm your body if taken for a long time. Drug labels often describe side effects and dangers. If a person notices serious side effects from a drug, he or she should talk to a doctor about them.

Some drugs—such as narcotics and others that affect the brain and nervous system—are sold illegally on the streets.

The only drugs safe to take are those given to you by your parents or doctors.

CAUTION: These drugs can be very dangerous. Never take a drug that is offered to you by a friend or acquaintance.

Modern drugs can indeed do wonderful things. They can cure and prevent many diseases. But they can also do serious harm. It is important to learn the facts about drugs, and to learn how to make wise decisions about drug use.

---

drum, *see* musical instrument

Dunes such as these in California are formed by winds blowing across the surface of the sand. Most dunes are found in deserts or along a coast.

dry cleaning

Dry cleaning is a way of cleaning cloth with little or no water. Instead, chemicals are used to remove stains. Some fabrics are dry-cleaned because washing would ruin them. For example, wool clothing often shrinks if washed in hot water. Some fabrics can be either washed or dry-cleaned. Others may be ruined by dry cleaning. In the United States, most clothing has labels that tell whether to wash or dry-clean.

At the dry cleaner, some spots are first removed by hand. Then the item is placed in a special washer with a chemical and sometimes a soap. Another machine spins the clothing to remove the fluid. Then the clothing is dried. Finally, the item is pressed or shaped. Delicate fabrics cannot go into the machines and must be dry-cleaned by hand.

Dry cleaning was invented in France in the mid-1800s. At first, there was danger of fire from the chemicals used. Now there are safer chemicals and better machines.

See also **soap; detergent;** and **clothing.**

duck, *see* water birds

dune

A dune is a hill of sand that forms where the wind usually blows in one direction. In the deserts of North Africa, the Middle East, and south-central Asia, thousands of square miles are covered by dunes. Dunes also form in wetter areas, such as the shores of Lake Michigan in North America.

Dunes have different shapes and sizes. In the Sahara, the great desert of North Africa, some dunes are more than 183 meters (600 feet) tall. A dune grows higher as the wind piles more grains of sand on it. In 40 years, a dune can grow 3 meters (10 feet).

The wind not only builds dunes, but moves them. Where winds blow steadily, a growing dune can travel more than 30 meters (100 feet) a year. As it travels, the dune may make strange booming sounds. These sounds are probably caused by falling sand.

There is a difference between the two sides of a dune. The side facing the wind is always longer and not so steep as the opposite side. The dune grows as wind blows sand up the long, sloping side. The dune moves because the sand gradually falls down the steep side.

See also **desert** and **sand.**

dye

Dyes are chemicals that are used to give something color. Most dyes are used on cloth. Dyes are also used to color ink, paper, hair, leather, and other things. The difference between dye and paint is that dyes soak into the material being dyed. Paints usually just cover the surface. (*See* **paint.**)

Most natural fibers—including cotton, wool, linen, and silk—are whitish, not really white. Man-made cloths—such as polyesters, nylons, and acrylics—do not start out brightly colored, either. Without dyes, people's clothes would all be grayish-white or brownish-white.

Have you ever wondered why most of the ancient Greeks and Romans are shown dressed in white clothes? One reason is that they did not have good, inexpensive dyes. They did know how to make a purple dye from shellfish found in the Mediterranean. But the purple dye was so prized that only the emperor and his family were allowed to use it.

Brightly dyed wool is hung out to dry in a street in Algeria.

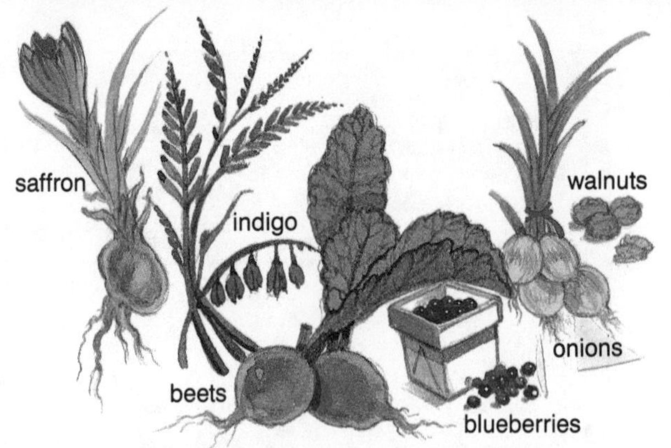

Some of the first dyes came from plants such as beets, onions, and berries.

Although royal purple came from shellfish, most early dyes were made from plants. Herbs such as woad, tansy, and madder were grown for the dyes that could be made from them. Woad, for example, produced a blue dye. It is famous as the dye that druids—pre-Christian priests—used to color their whole bodies blue. (*See* **Celts.**)

Later, dyes were made from minerals. The metal chromium, named after the Greek word for "color," appears in dyes named chrome yellow, chrome red, and chrome green. The best red dye was made from tiny insects. One kilogram (2¼ pounds) of the red dye required 200,000 of the insects.

The problem with many of these natural dyes is that they are not very "fast." Fast dyes do not fade quickly when exposed to sunlight or after being laundered, dried, and ironed. Their colors should last a long time. Modern dyes that are very fast are mostly synthetic—made from chemicals instead of natural materials.

The first synthetic dye was produced in 1856 by an 18-year-old English boy, William Perkin. He learned how to make a shade of purple from coal. The dye and the color it produced were called *mauve.* Mauve quickly became so popular that the next few years are known as the "Mauve Decade" in England. The success of mauve led to the discovery of new dyes in coal and other substances. Among these were magenta, and new forms of green, black, and red.

See also **color** and **clothmaking.**

dynamite, *see* explosive